BRADFORD'S
ROCK 'N' ROLL

by

Derek A J Lister

BRADFORD'S

ROCK 'N' ROLL

— the Golden Years

(1959 - 1965)

by

Derek A J Lister

Bradford Libraries and Information Service

First Published in 1991
Bradford Libraries and Information Service

Text © Derek A J Lister 1991

ISBN 0-907734-26-X

Typeset in Garamond by Primary Colour, Bradford
Printed by Smiths Colour Printers, Bradford
Cover design by Kate Mellalieu

CONTENTS

PREFACE
by Mike Priestley

What a tremendous time it was to be young, as the 1950s rocked on into the 1960s. There was never an era like it before, and there will never be one again. It was a time when to be young was to find yourself as part of a new generation of people who were neither children nor adults. Before teenagers were invented, with their own music and fashions, lads went straight from school uniforms into suits like their dads wore and lasses soon began to look more or less like their mums.

But then came rock 'n' roll, and everything changed. The cult of youth began and quickly established its heroes: rebels like James Dean, frantic rock 'n' rollers like Little Richard and Jerry Lee Lewis, mean and moody Elvis, even the middle-aged-looking Bill Haley whose invitation to Rock Around the Clock prompted the Teds to smash many a cinema around the country for reasons best known to themselves.

It was a time when the young, strongly encouraged by commercial interests, began to follow their own clothing fashions — often much to the dismay of their parents. Many a household saw ugly confrontations between strait-laced fathers and sons sporting sideburns, drape jackets, drainpipe trousers and bootlace ties, or daughters with powdered faces, crimson lipstick, tight blouses and flouncy skirts worn over half a dozen underskirts. And many a parent bellowed "TURN THAT RUBBISH OFF!" as Dansettes blasted out as best they could the rock 'n' roll sounds which had been denounced in America as "the devil's music".

What fantasies we pimply adolescents nurtured, standing in front of mirrors with combs in our hands to act as pretend microphones and singing along with Elvis, or Gene Vincent, or Billy Fury (who became one of my particular heroes after someone on Blackpool Prom said I looked like him, which I did in a poor light if a combed my hair into a Fury quiff, turned-up my collar and hunched my shoulders).

During that period, Liverpool was nurturing the musical talent which was to burst on to the rock scene in the early 1960s and give that city a reputation which will stay with it forever, despite the hard times it has gone through since.

But much was happening in Bradford, too. There was talent a-plenty growing up amid what were then still dark satanic mills. Just how much talent I never realised until, a couple of years ago, I interviewed Derek Lister about his years as disc-jockey Dal Stevens at the Majestic and the Gaumont and later met a bunch of one-time members of such legendary Bradford groups (which is what bands used to be called) as the Cresters and the Dingos before they played a hugely successful reunion gig.

The hundreds who turned up to hear them at the Pile Bar could have been hundreds of thousands at Wembley Stadium, perhaps, if Brian Epstein had owned a record shop in Bradford instead of in Liverpool and had decided to manage the groups which were working the clubs and pubs and dance halls round here.

That would have been a very different story for Derek Lister to tell. However, the reality makes fascinating reading. He's done a splendid job of presenting an insider's-eye view of an exciting period in Bradford's recent history and reminding us of that golden era when life was full of fun and optimism and rock 'n' roll.

Read on, and rock on . . . . .

ACKNOWLEDGEMENTS

The contents of this book have been compiled from memory, recollections going back twenty-five years. A ceaseless motivation has been required and, without the help of the following, senility would have crept in and prevented me from completing it. Certain information which could have been of assistance was not forthcoming, but in the main, people were most helpful.

Our local newspaper the *Telegraph & Argus* helped instigate my first interview, although many of the photgraphs taken by them at this time are no longer in existence; a sad loss of Bradford's heritage.

First of all I wish to express my deepest gratitude to my wife Diana who kept my many mundane but harrowing problems at arm's length. During the writing of this book she also weathered my foul temper, artistic pretentions, and endless torments; herself overcoming my unorthodox use of the Queen's English. From what looked like early scripts of *The Goon Show*, she corrected, edited and typed, creating, hopefully, something quite readable.

Also, thanks go to my daughter Angelique for her pre-typing work, and Michelle Jepson Smith for helping bring the manuscript to some order.

My grateful thanks to the ever popular Mike Priestley, reporter, columnist and Devil's disciple of the *Telegraph & Argus*. I feel he, above most, deserves a special mention, as without his original interview followed by a splendid feature article on my D.J. days I could not have found the motivation to continue my writing. I was completely inspired and encouraged to "follow that!" His article in the *Telegraph & Argus* resulted in many long lost colleagues of the 60s pop world contacting me, who in turn gave a hand in pointing me in the right direction. My sincere thanks to Mike for his assistance and a special thanks to him for writing the preface.

Thanks also to Dorothy Box of Pennine Radio, Melvin Blossom of BBC Radio Leeds, both of whom interviewed me on the radio which assisted in the collation of information from former Sixties groups and Rock 'n' Rollers of that time. Special thanks are also extended to the two former members of my old group, Keith Artist and Dennis 'Duane' Oliver, whose useful visits to my home helped stimulate my memory for facts and dates that otherwise would have escaped me.

For help with the photography of some of the early groups, my thanks to Andrew Artist. A very special thanks to Graham Harrison (the well-known authority on Buddy Holly and The Crickets) who kindly loaned me some of the autographed photographs originally in my own collection.

Very special thanks to Bob Duckett, Senior Librarian (Reference Services), of Bradford Libraries, without whose enthusiasm and help this book would not have been published. This gentleman's patient encouragement and advice has ensured that the details herein are a unique reference to the history of Bradford's Rock 'n' Roll era between 1959-65.

Many thanks also to Sally Wolfe, again from Bradford Libraries, whose many suggestions and careful organisation and publicity skills have helped expedite this accurate and well documented Rock 'n' Roll handbook. And to Kate Mellalieu, the Libraries' Display Artist, who read my mind and brought to life the book cover, creating a truly professional and bright finish.

Sincere thanks to the many local group members of yesteryear who contacted me and loaned their treasured photographs, together with notes and well remembered data. Most of them showing eagerness and excitement at the thought of having their cherished teenage memories rekindled in the form of this book. Almost twenty five years had passed when I met again with most of them, but the eyes and minds were clear as these near-middle-aged men recalled and reflected on those never-to-be-forgotten days of long ago.

Most of the photographs used in this book are my property, or have been loaned to me to use. In addition I wish to thank Geoff Mellor and Bill Preedy for permission to use three illustrations from their book *The Cinemas of Bradford*; Mrs Bruce of the Bradford Photographic Survey; Bradford Libraries and Information Service; the *Telegraph & Argus;* and Kiki Dee.

A very big thank you to you all.

Derek A J Lister, 1991

PROLOGUE

For the last twenty-five years I have been going to write this book, now I find I must, as memories fade. I was also embarrassed into motivation by being made to look and feel inferior by the 1980s so-called DJ (have deck — will travel type) recently at a friend's party. On arrival the usual five hundred decibels were pounding the room. The sound was coming from what I thought was NASA Control consisting of flashing lights, dials, knobs, dual turntables, etc. All that was required was 'We have lift off' and the scene would have been complete. Looming at the back of the MGM set was the 'Disc Jockey'.

Three points told me he was the disc jockey; one, where he stood in his module; two, his large 'Dunlop tyre'-type looking earphones; and three, an inaudible noise resounding through the microphone. Conversation was useless when trying to speak to people you had not seen for years, so at the end of the evening you would still not know any more about them than when you last saw them before. It is always during the few seconds break when changing records that the conversation endeavours to take place, some-times to no avail. It was during one of these pauses that I made my way across to the Lunar Module to proudly claim that I, many years ago, was a Disc Jockey. This I did at the same time as asking "How does this machine work?" He mumbled something I could not catch, thrust one of the large Dunlop tyres to my ear, I thought I could hear Radio Luxembourg; he then quite rudely looked me up and down and nonchalantly retreated to his 'your looking good' syndrome. All this and £50.00 too! I returned to my seat in the corner, this being the furthest point from the Space Centre, and reflected that for six years during the Golden Age of Rock 'n' Roll, I had been part of a scene that would never return.

During that time, from 1959 to 1965, I had met stars and would-be stars; most of whom I would eventually end up on first name terms with. I also had my own Rock Group, playing the local scene with many other local groups. The odd one did have some success nationally, whilst myself and numerous others were 'also-rans', who made up the local scene, but who also had a wealth of talent.

Cash rewards were almost non-existent and hardly covered expenses. But, I believe, like most of my colleagues with whom I have been in contact during the process of writing this book . . . we enjoyed it!

In the following pages I have tried to put together a picture of Bradford's Rock Scene, especially of the Gaumont and Majestic Dance Hall venues during the late Fifties until the mid-Sixties. I will try and name names when and where required, omissions may be made, but not always intentionally, so I hope my colleagues from those great days, plus the more astute Rock 'n' Roll fans, will forgive any omissions or mistakes.

During my research it has become very apparent that there is a need to record something of our very own local groups, who, through this period, gave immeasurable pleasure to thousands of young people from Bradford and the surrounding districts. Bradford had a wealth of talent — vocalists, guitarists, and drummers — who compared favourably with the top groups of the country. The local groups exported this talent to other parts of the country, and in some cases nationally, but they were never recognised with a title like the 'Bradford', or the 'Yorkshire Sound'. The 'Mersey Sound' had a title which could not be removed. Most groups over the border seemed to acquire some success while our own talented groups never achieved the fame which most of them richly deserved. In writing this book I have met and renewed friendships with many ex-members of these groups. In doing so I decided that they were as much a part of the Bradford scene as I was. In fact, even more so. Who had heard of 'Dal Stevens' outside Bradford? But many will have heard of Mike Sagar and His Cresters in other regions. Therefore, I have tried to include as many of the groups and other personalities who made up Bradford's Rock 'n' Roll scene during 1959-65 as I can. In most cases I have been able to obtain original photographs — to bring the memories flooding back and to be a tribute to all those who took part in this adventure. Some recognition is truly deserved.

For those who took part in the adventure, whether it was at the Gaumont, Majestic, Students' Club, or elsewhere, this must bring you to your mid forties, at least. Perhaps you can recognise yourself again all those years ago and say "Yes! I certainly remember that!" It may be nostalgia, but nostalgia of a type we shall never see again. If you notice, it's still the records of those days that start the foot tapping. For the young ones of today, who look at Mums and Dads and say "Who?" when a name like Eden Kane is mentioned, this might be a small insight into the Rock 'n' Roll scene in the Bradford of their Mum and Dad's time all those years ago, and perhaps it might help them to understand why we look back to those days so nostalgically.

Derek A J Lister Alias 'Dal Stevens' 1991

Rock 'n' Roll

"It was a revolution. It changed the lives of a generation. It spread across the world. It scared authority rigid, forced the adult world to reassess itself. Most remarkable of all, for something so profound, it was a revolution without blood. Rock 'n' Roll changed everything if you were a teen in the Fifties. They way you looked, the way you talked, the way you dressed, the way you walked, the way you danced. It changed the way you looked at the world, at authority, at your parents. But most of all it changed the way you looked at yourself. Before Rock 'n' Roll, youth between the ages of 12 and 20 had been either overgrown kids or cut-down adults. Either way they had conformed to their parents view of themselves. They had dressed in imitation of their parents, and, generally shared their tastes. Rock 'n' Roll wiped that out. Rock 'n' Roll created a separate tribe, with its own rituals, its own uniform, its own mysteries, its own language, its own music. Rock 'n' Roll created teenagers. An extraordinary, raucous, crude, shouted music, charged with energy and driven by a manic crushing pulse. You can hear it and feel it, But you cannot break it down and analyse it. Rock 'n' Roll more than any other popular music defies intellectual examination."

Jeremy Pascall *'The Illustrated History of Rock Music'*
2nd Ed. Hamlyn, 1984

CHAPTER ONE
The Early Days

Ientered the Rock 'n' Roll era at the beginning; being one of those lucky ones to be just seventeen in the mid-Fifties,when Elvis's *Blue Suede Shoes* and *Hound Dog* were prominent in the Hit Parade; and so called hooligans were ripping up cinema seats to Bill Haley's *Rock Around The Clock.* These were the days of 'Teddy Boys', lemon socks, 2″ crepe soled shoes, string ties, 12″ bottoms, velvet collars and the Tony Curtis hairstyle (affectionately known as the DA). Thus equipped, you were entitled to partake in the world of Rock 'n' Roll.

My first introduction to this world was at the Queen's, at Idle. Looking back, this seemed rather a small place. It had very subdued

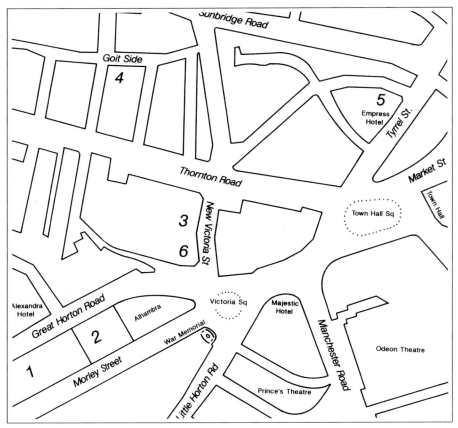

Bradford in the early 1960s. Design by Kate Mellalieu.

1. *Kings and Queens Halls Ball Room;*
2. *Majestic Dance Hall;*
3. *Gaumont Ballroom;*
4. *Southgate (Co-op Hall);*
5. *Gaiety Dance Hall;*
6. *Students Club*

lighting, but a fair amount of volume coming from the speakers, and no Disc Jockey. The room was wall-to-wall with people, making it hot, humid and sticky. The slow numbers ('Ballads') such as Sam Cooke's *Ivory Tower*, were ideal for a smooch and chatting up the girls, but it was at the Queen's that I found out that the fast numbers for jiving or bopping to were not for me. Not only did I find that I hadn't much rhythm, but also that I was sweating profusely within seconds, then having to make some excuse, leave the floor, look for air and dry off. Try making conversation with water running off your chin and nose! So for the next few years I became one of the many males who spent most of the evening sitting these numbers out.

For 1/- (5p) admission, plus bus fares, it wasn't a bad night out. It was also the time of the dance bands, and such venues as Bert Shutts, Textile Hall, Gaiety, Gaumont and Co-op Hall. But these were still more or less Modern Ballroom Dancing for which the writing was on the wall, and by the mid-Sixties these would be long gone.

It was during the two years while in the army that I learnt to absorb more and more of Rock 'n' Roll. The wireless was our only real contact with the outside world, so Radio Luxembourg was a must, plus the odd TV *Six-Five Specials*. During this time Gene Vincent became my hero; never at that time thinking that in a few years I would be in his company many times and on first name terms.

On leaving the Forces in 1958 I made new friends, and during some of our nights out I would do my rendering of the *Rock Island Line* and *John Henry,* Lonnie Donegan's skiffle numbers. This got to be hard work after a time because everywhere we went it was demanded, not by the general public, but by my so-called friends who would shout "He can sing!", pointing their fingers at me. My face would change to the usual colour of the embarrassed, and I would mutter, "No, I can't sing", but to no avail, as in the next few seconds I would find myself with a pianist, who could not play, just as I could not sing - or could I?

Because, as time went on I began to like it, although still embarrassed, I found myself asking for the mike (microphone), and could I sing another? At the end of these so-called numbers, people would applaud, or that's what I thought they did! Whether it was the amount of alcohol absorbed I don't know, but it felt good, and gave me the confidence to take the next step, which was to form a group.

'SOMERSET' PRIVATE SCHOOL OF DANCING

11 Idle Road, Undercliffe, Bradford. Phone .9376

MEMBER'S CARD

PRIVATE CLASSES FOR DANCE PRACTICE

Clifford Dutton

NOT TRANSFERABLE

"QUEENS" BALLROOM

SUNDAY CLUB

MEMBERS CARD

PRIVATE CLASSES FOR DANCE PRACTICE

CLIFFORD DUTT..

Phone Idle 1238 NOT TRANSFERABLE

CHAPTER TWO
Dal Is Born

How do you form a group? I would not like to try today, but in the late Fifties it was comparatively easy. Why? Because if you were not an art student, then you were in a group. Why do I say art student? Well, it seemed in the Bradford of those days, in the coffee bars and dance halls, everyone appeared to be an art student at Bradford Tech. It's a wonder we had anyone else for other careers! Where have they all gone?

One of my friends was Terence Moran. We were very much alike in most things, having been at school together (St Patrick's, Westgate, known affectionately in those days as White Abbey College, being in the vicinity of White Abbey Flats). On leaving school we had both joined Brown Muffs, now Rackhams, as young sales assistants. We left the store when we were called up for National Service and, once again, ended up together in the same regiment. So it was on demobilisation in 1958 that we once more renewed our friendship in civvy street. Terry had taken piano lessons which made him quite an artiste in a jazzy sort of way, so when we had our nights out with the lads, we used to get together, Terry on the piano and I would do the vocal. We only knew a couple of numbers, namely Lonnie Donegan's *John Henry* and Presley's *Blue Suede Shoes*. In spite of this, we decided to form a group. This was in the summer of 1959.

The group was to include Mike Farrell (another old school friend) on bass guitar; Doug Lamb, lead guitar; Sam Flaherty, rhythm guitar; and a young fifteen year old drummer called 'Keg'. Why 'Keg'? to this day I really don't know! Our only equipment was a small 15 watt amplifier (no mike) which meant we could only plug in the lead guitarist. The others just gave as much unamplified sound as possible. Having a pianist in the group always caused problems, because if we had a booking or even just wanted to practice, we had to have a piano and they were not easy to come by. Luckily we were able to make some use of Doug Lamb's house, his mother offering us the front room for practice, which had the required piano. Practices always seemed short and sometimes a waste of time. Try it sometime — six teenagers trying to blend some accord in music, temperament, ability and patience, while trying not to be too loud in case it offended the neighbours! Then, of course, what do we call ourselves (apart from the obvious)? In those days names did not seem to matter too much, as you were either a pair, a trio, the Four . . . ., the Five . . . ., or Fred Nirk and the Goons. In our case we decided to call ourselves the Blue Jays. 'Blue' because we would all wear blue ties (Slim Jims), which gave us some kind of identity (not being able to afford matching suits), and 'Jays' because it sounded different. Looking back, I cannot imagine why anyone would want to be called a Blue Jay, but being young and impressionable, and also daft at the time, it sounded real. My name would also be in lights, 'Dal Stevens' DAL - my initials, that was an easy one. Then to get Stevens we sifted through thousands of surnames trying to get the right balance, something that would roll off the tongue with the Blue Jays. Someone had already got to the top name Presley, so it had to be Stevens. We were now formed as a group, Dal Stevens and the Blue Jays.

With practice we produced a repertoire of some of the popular numbers of the time. A few that come to mind are: *Be-Bop-A-Lula, It'll be me, Blue Suede Shoes, Whole lot a shakin' goin' on, I go ape, Tallahasi Lassie, Chantilly Lace, Dream, Southern Love, Teenager in Love.* Now we are rar-ing to go; to take Bradford by storm; to be discovered; to play *Sunday Night at the London Palladium.* All we required now was a booking.

Our first venue came through some friends who were members of the Young Conservatives and, on finding out we were looking for a trial, offered us the opportunity to play after a Young Conservative's Dinner at the Connaught Rooms on Manningham Lane. Being the brilliant organiser I was, I never bothered to find out if there would be the main essentials that would be required for a top group, ie, plug sockets, mike and, of course, the proverbial piano. The result was that our first gig was a flop. We could never have contem-plated such a happening as we set off full of enthusiasm for the Connaught Rooms. Terry had a Ford Consul car in which he picked up Keg with his drums. The rest of us made our way by bus, dressed in our best suits, spotless white shirts and our blue ties, convinced that everyone would recognise us as the Blue Jays. On arrival we were shown to an oak panelled room that was adjacent to the dining room. It was in this room that the Young Conservatives would file after being sustained by an ample meal and a few "shorts". Our first objective was to set up our equipment, which was our fifteen watt amplifier and drum kit. At one end of the room was a grand piano, which we were thankful for, because we never asked when we accepted the booking if there was one, so on reflection this was a stroke of luck. The only trouble was that the piano was at one end of the room and the socket (where we would plug the amplifier) was at the other, the distance between the two being some thirty yards. This meant that Terry would be seated at the piano at one end of the room while the three guitarists and drummer were at the other end plugged into the fifteen watt amplifier, and I, the vocalist, would be stood like a prawn on my own in the centre of the room!

The biggest shock to my system was finding out that there was no microphone, in fact, no sound system at all. This again showed a lack of experience for not checking if there was a piano, sockets, microphone, etc. I could have wept. My first, sorry *our* first booking! But, as they say, the show must go on.

The Young Conservatives sidled in with drinks in hands, to mingle among us until I couldn't see anything of Terry at one end of the room, nor the rest of the Blue Jays at the other side of the room. So while all these people stood over and around me, I went into the first number which was Gene Vincent's *Be-Bop-A-Lula*. I could not sing, I had to shout, the piano was banging away at one side of the room, three guitarists strumming and one drummer belting it out at the other side. Needless to say, nobody heard me. It was a competition who could make the most noise. This happened through all our numbers. Even so, at the end of each rendition the crowd politely clapped, more out of sympathy, plus the heavy consumption of alcohol. They were happy, they were enjoying themselves, while I was wishing the ground would open up and swallow me! I don't know who decided to call it a day, whether it was them or us, but someone had to give in, and I didn't care any more, my voice had nearly gone. Luckily we called it a day in unison.

You could imagine what the audience was like, someone was asking Terry if he could play any classical numbers on the piano to which I believe he gave some negative reply. As we packed our equipment away the organiser of the dinner came to me and said how good we were and he would like us back for a further venue in the near future. Thirty years on and I'm still awaiting the return booking, although, to be fair, he did pay our fee of one guinea - £1.05 - for six of us. Again that was inexperience, the going rate was two or three guineas, so at today's prices we were paid about eighteen pence each. This experience would have been enough to put anyone off for life. But although disappointed, it had taught us a lesson, showing us our deficiencies and lack of experience. We could only learn from this, our first booking!

After this fiasco we had to organise ourselves into promoting the group: having cards printed, spreading the word, and, of course, getting bookings. Nothing really big came along that was exciting, only the occasional small clubs at three guineas a time, which meant that we were really a non-profit-making organisation, as costs of transporting drums — bus fares — did not leave much change out of ten shillings each.

Once we played at the reception of a friend's wedding. To think we made ourselves available free of charge, with people at the reception complaining we were too loud, while young children ran about causing havoc. The older generation made the usual drunken remarks about the group, and budding Perry Como's wanted to take over the mike — you've seen and heard them. This type of venue we never did again, learning another lesson.

At last we were given the opportunity of what was classed the best booking in the area, The Bradford Top Rank Majestic Dance Hall. I had been going to the 'Majestic' on Saturday for the 'Modern Dancing' scene. This was the old Morley Street Picture House. It had been re-developed into a dance hall in the late Fifties, with dancing every night to "Billy Hey and His Orchestra", admission 2/6. This was not really the teenage scene, more the early twenties-plus age group.

Mr Lawrance was the manager during this time. He was the original English gentleman who was always courteous and well respected by both modern and teenage patrons. It was during my Saturday Modern Dance visit that I mentioned to Mr Lawrance that I had recently formed a group, and he then suggested we have a spot on the Monday Rock 'n' Roll session.

Laurie Lawrance. The original English Gentleman, Manager of the Majestic Ballroom.

Generally billed as the guest group, it would be for two twenty-minute spots between the disc sessions. The Disc Jockey, I remember, seemed to be one of Billy Hey's Orchestra; to this day I do not know what his name was. With this forthcoming booking it would mean having to practice more and also extend our repertoire as we still only had a few numbers. Two twenty-minute spots made an average of sixteen numbers, eight for each session. One thing with instrumental numbers was that you could drag them out, which would help pass the time. We also had to take into consideration that the teenagers had really come to dance, so this meant giving them something with a beat — no ballads. Ballads are for people who have come to listen (and smooch) not dance.

Ballads, I found, caused trouble. People stood around, fidgeted and conversed. The troublemakers were waiting for that out-of-tune note that always came, and this in turn would cause jeering or some obscene remark, thus putting the ballad singer off. In doing so you had lost control of the crowd out there, so, especially being new, no ballads. Later, during my career with the group, and as a Disc Jockey, I saw quite a few groups lose face with this problem.

We had our first recognised booking and were billed in the *Telegraph and Argus* (see adverts on page 10) as a guest group with popular numbers, The Blue Jays.

The Monday came and we made our way by bus, with Terry again bringing Keg and Drums in his car. We arrived about 7.00 pm and were greeted by Mr Lawrence who introduced us to the DJ who gave us our times, which were 8-15 to 8.35 pm and 9.30 to 9.50 pm. It goes without saying that the Majestic had a piano on the stage. This being for Billy Hey's Orchestra, and also a marvellous PA system. We still had only our fifteen watt amplifier which two of our guitarists could plug into, but at least I had a microphone which would make us sound a little better. It also meant that when I wasn't singing I could put the microphone by the piano to give more volume.

GAUMONT BALLROOM	GAUMONT BALLROOM	DANCING
TONIGHT.	TONIGHT.	MAJESTIC BALLROOM
BIG BEAT NITE	BIG BEAT NITE.	MODERN DANCING EVERY EVENING.
Rock 'n Roll to top discs —plus your favourite Groups.	Rock 'n Roll to Top Discs.	MON.: Teenage Night, R 'n' R Session
This Week's Guests: Dal Stevens and the Four Jukes and the Casa-Mians.	PLUS	Favourite Records, 7.30—10.30, 2/-.
7.30—10.30.	THE DAL STEVENS GROUP.	Guest Group with Popular Numbers
Adm. 2/-.	7.30—10.30. Adm. 1/9.	"THE BLUE JAYS."

Adverts in the Telegraph & Argus Winter 1959-60

Dressed in our usual suits with our blue ties, we were shown to the dressing room, down the stairs at the right hand side of the stage. I was to see a lot of that dressing room in the next few years, but at that particular moment I had to admit I was rather scared. The other venues were nothing compared with this, the difference being we would be appearing in front of nearly a thousand teenagers who could be very critical. The young ones of that period knew their records and the stars who performed them and, as most groups copied the popular numbers of the time, it was easy to spot any mistakes, so you had to sound like the original as much as possible.

In the dressing room we joked and smoked as the time moved on to 8.15 pm. All we could hear was the DJ's announcements, and then the sounds of the records, but most disturbing was the impact of 1,000 pairs of feet thumping from the ballroom floor. This bounded through the dressing room, creating a condemned man's environment. At 8.15 pm we were ushered by the DJ onto the stage. The stage was open with no curtain. This meant we had to file onto the stage, and with people staring at us, it was no time to have an inferiority complex. On stage Mike, Sam and Doug did the usual tuning up of guitars. Terry sat himself at the piano, and Keg slid onto his drum seat. As for myself, I sauntered around the centre of the stage trying to give the impression that I was the No. 1 star. At last the DJ's record came to an end and then we were introduced as 'Del Stevens and the Blue Jays', note the Del. On his introduction the crowd went wild, or did it? I seem to remember the odd clap, the usual obscene remark came floating up to the stage, a one, two, three, and off we went into Gene Vincent's *Be-Bop-A-Lula*. After finishing this number, again came the odd applause and shouts, so into the next song we went, an instrumental, the Shadow's number *Apache*. We got through seven numbers before the DJ was back on stage nodding our time was almost up, and this would be our last number this session.

Off we went, back to the dressing room and the condemned cell, with another hour to pass, to await the 9.30 pm session. We did not dare venture out of the dressing room as we thought of the criticisms that would be levelled at us if we left our safe haven. The hour passed, then we were back on stage for our next eight numbers. This half went a lot better as we were now more confident. Again the DJ appeared around our seventh number, giving us a thumbs up, time to go. I signed off after this number, acknowledging the same sporadic applause saying I hoped we would be back soon. Someone shouted "Not if they could help it!"

On our return to the dressing room I was asked if I would call at Mr Lawrance's office for our payment, which was four guineas. Mr Lawrance, with his usual diplomatic aplomb, greeted me by saying we were quite good, some adjustments were required, but, in saying this, he went to his diary and gave us two further Monday night bookings. This was Mr Lawrance, always willing to give advice and install confidence to the younger generation. So our first real booking had been, as far as we were concerned, quite a success. We had played in front of a large crowd, no problems, and had been given two further bookings. On our get together the following night, we agreed where our problems lay, but most of all we had been given confidence. Thanks to this booking we were hoping for success as one of the top groups in the area, even Britain! But things were not to be.

CHAPTER THREE
Aim For Fame

With the two bookings we had obtained from the Majestic and the occasional club we were not, at that stage, doing too badly considering we were all working lads. But this meant making sure that the six of us could rendezvous at the same time and place for each engagement. Having no transport of our own meant using public transport. We could not afford to hire a vehicle because, firstly, we were not being paid enough to warrant the cost, and secondly, public transport was, after all, cheaper. So reluctantly, we had to observe this method. Try it sometime! Organise six young men to be at the other side of Bradford for 7.00 pm with drums and other equipment, with the inducement of playing three hours for 15/- each (75p). It would not work today. In those days it did because we enjoyed it - the money wasn't essential, but it did help. We had now savoured playing before crowds of a few hundred, so our next step was to play before a few thousand; as people used to say in those days "When are you going to be on *The London Palladium*?" You had really reached the top when asked to appear on *The Palladium,* a Sunday night TV show hosted by Bruce Forsyth. So, like all would-be's, we had our ambitions.

One short cut, or so it seemed at the time, was to audition for a show at the Alhambra called *Aim for Fame.* This was similar to *Opportunity Knocks.* Some impressario would hire a theatre like the Alhambra and would audition the local talent, then have nights of each contesting the other. On the Saturday there would be a final, the prizes being £25 for 1st, £15 2nd, £10 3rd. I made the usual approaches for consideration, which found us a week later in a queue outside the Alhambra for the said audition.

The usual contestants mingled amongst us, the Shirley Temples, Ronnie Hiltons, Marvo the Magicians, and Grimaldi the Jugglers etc, etc. Surprisingly, we had not long to wait and were soon ushered in and asked to set up our equipment on stage. We did so quickly, and were soon ready. The spotlights shone right on to the centre of the stage, so we could not see anything, only the rising of expensive cigar smoke through the spotlight ray, which told us someone was down there giving judgement.

"Right," said the voice from the smoke, "Play away". So with that rather unusual introduction off we went, one, two, three "Come on pretty baby let's move it and groove it" (Cliff Richard's *Move It*), That's as far as we reached when the smoker's voice said "Enough, go and see Miss Whatever". Miss Whatever was at the side of the stage with clipboard in hand. She asked for the full name of our group and said we would be in the first round on Monday. So, we were through.

I thought it best to make some enquiries as to who the judges might be, local celebrities? television-film stars? who? Then I found out it was to be none of these, it was definitely like an *Opportunity Knocks* competition. The winners would be selected by audience applause. This meant trying to get as many relations as possible down on the night, to help the clapometer get you through. On further investigation, I found that practically everyone who auditioned got through. This, of course, would swell the box office receipts and bring financial success to the organisers, if not to the contestants! We were again appearing free of charge!

The following Monday saw us installed in a dressing room in the Alhambra. They were minute, and in most cases, shared. Our companion was a budding David Whitfield. Probably in his mid-forties, he spent most of the time boasting about where and who he had appeared with. He kept sneaking to the corner for a quick swig from a very large hipflask which appeared to have a never ending quantity of alcohol. We sarcastically laughed at him and threw in the odd cynical remark, which, on reflection, was not clever and most unkind, but we were young and smart, and trying for the top. He was actually billed to go on before us but pleaded with us to go on before him. This we did. At least with our equipment we could set this up behind the curtain while another turn was on the front of the stage. An impressionist was going through an Arthur Askey routine.

On hearing him finish, I heard the same sporadic applause I had heard at the Majestic. Was it the same crowd? No, it couldn't be, as I knew my parents would be out there, as would Terry's, Mike's, Keg's, Doug's and Sam's, plus all our friends and relations. The impressionist shuffled off and in seconds the compere had introduced us from in front of the curtain. The said curtain hurtled back and there we were exposed to the world, transfixed, and blinded in a fierce beam of light, unable to see a single soul in the audience. But we knew they were out there as the atmosphere was electric. Our first number was *A Whole lot a shakin' goin' on* and we gave it everything we'd got. A-one, two, a-one, two, three, four — away we went. This was a number we thought we did quite well, and it was a foot tapper, which even the older generation appreciated. On conclusion there was quite a generous applause from all our families and relations, thus ensuring us a place in the next round. Logically, we would be through with generous applause, as the organisers would almost certainly want this contingent at the next round, ensuring more patrons, meaning financial success!

At the semi-final on Thursday there was a repeat of the previous Monday. This time we had our own dressing room. No imitation David Whitfields to share with. Incidentally, he never followed us on stage that Monday, he just disappeared. Again, all our relations were present, ensuring a place in the final on Saturday. So now we had our chance. Even if we got third prize it would help our financial embarrassment.

At that particular time most of the turns in the finals were groups or singers. Two of the groups were The Dingos and Rhythm Rebels and as they were more organised and professional than ourselves, I knew we were up against stiff opposition. We went through the usual procedure and it was almost as if we had been doing this all our lives, so, even if we did not win, we certainly knew we were gaining valuable experience.

On the night we were good, but not good enough, as both the Rhythm Rebels and The Dingos far outclassed us. We thought that they were big-headed and looked down on us, but this was sour grapes on our behalf, as they were really far better both musically and with their presentation, but it did not stop us feeling resentful.

This, of course, did not last. As time went on all the local groups became very good friends and could be said to have a cult following over that period.

During the competition, one contestant had been overlooked by most of us. This was a young fourteen year old girl who had a tremendous voice and talent. Her name was Pauline Matthews. In the packed house of *Aim for Fame,* Pauline Matthews was first, The Dingos were second. Dal Stevens and the Blue Jays did not get a look in. It had to be, as we never got to the top, but Pauline Matthews did, alias Kiki Dee.

Pauline Matthews (Kiki Dee) in 1969. (Telegraph & Argus, 24 Sept 1977).
(Photo courtesy of Kiki Dee)

Incidentally, the third prize went to another of Bradford's female vocalists, Josie McCann, with the Connie Frances hit number *Lipstick on your collar!* Alas, Josie did not follow in the footsteps of Kiki Dee. A shame really as she also had a wealth of talent that could have been developed on similar lines to those of Kiki Dee.

We came in frequent contact with The Dingos during this period and we all began to feel that Terry was not too happy with the situation and was setting his sights higher — namely to join The Dingos, and we were not so naive as to not realise that Garth Cawood, leader of The Dingos had made approaches to Terry to join them. He had said he would consider the offer.

As well as the Majestic bookings, we secured an eight week booking at the Co-op Hall, Southgate, every Wednesday, called the *Two Shilling Hop*. This was a good booking at £5, plus useful publicity leaflets. Even the tickets had our name on, which made us quite popular. This venue gave us the opportunity to experiment with numbers, which gave us an insight as to whether the teenagers liked or disliked the music by their response. Thus we could keep a number in as the crowd suggested, or discard it.

The Co-op Hall has long since been demolished; a shame really for it was a good sound building with a large stage and a good PA system. It was a popular venue as it was pretty central, just off Thornton Road, and quite easy to get to. The crowds were not as large as the Majestic, probably around 450, mostly the same patrons turning up each week, but like most teenagers of the time, likeable and enthusiastic, helping make the Wednesday nights very successful. At that time we were performing Mondays at the Majestic, Wednesdays at the *Two Shilling Hop* at the Co-op Hall, and the odd weekend at Working Men's Clubs; so we decided we would make a record, or what was called a 'demo-disc'. This was a disc we could send to agents to obtain more bookings. or even a recording contract.

Some who heard us play in those days will say "What a cheek, they were rubbish!" but I'd heard worse. Anyway, what had we got to lose? The

CO-OP HALL — SOUTHGATE — BRADFORD

HEY! CATS! HEARD THE NEWS?

JIVE   BE-BOP   ROCK 'N ROLL

EVERY WEDNESDAY AT THE CO-OP HALL, SOUTHGATE

EVERYBODY'S WELCOME AT THE

2/- HOP
7-30 to 10-30

FEATURING

DAL. STEVENS with the BLUE J's

AND ALL THE LATEST RECORDS

Publicity Handout for an eight week booking.

CO-OP HALL · SOUTHGATE · BRADFORD

2/—
HOP

Dancing to
DAL STEVENS *with the*
BLUE J's Rock 'n Roll Group

augmented by all the latest records
7-30 to 10-30

THIS TICKET IS AVAILABLE FOR   2 1 OCT 1959

A ticket to see the Blue Jays.

cost was £1 for the master and 10/- for each copy; and that was for an A and B side. The establishment in which this momentous event was to take place was in Shipley, namely Excel Records. We made the venue on Saturday afternoon in early 1960. We had chosen not to play over Christmas, so for a few weeks we had been conscientiously practising and trying to organise ourselves for the New Year. In this break we would 'cut a disc'. As usual our caravan made its way independently to the said studios. The building had a shop frontage and upstairs, in a huge former lounge, we found ourselves setting up our somewhat primitive equipment: drums, fifteen watt amplifier, etc. I had checked that a piano was available, so my organising skills were improving! The walls of the room were covered with egg boxes in place of wall paper. And these were wall-to-wall, as well as to the ceiling. This gave a certain sound proofing to the room and made it into a cosy, silent studio. Later I knew members of the groups who did this in their own bedroom, to appease mothers/fathers, and especially neighbours. Excel Studios had some really fantastic equipment in way of microphones and sound boxes, which made it appear very professional compared to our novice approach. The gentleman whose business it was, organised us into some order, tested for sound, and disappeared behind a small glass panel and began miming and gesticulating wildly, then thumbs up, to proceed.

For this occasion it was only logical that we chose the best two numbers we were able to execute, or thought we did best; the A-side would be Jerry Lee Lewis's *A Whole Lot A Shakin' Goin' On*. For this we had the piano and it helped because the number was 75% made up of Jerry Lee Lewis's unique style of playing.

As we proceeded during the recording, I had arranged during the number that I would introduce each member of the group, who would then proceed to do some small solo on their particular instrument. This took place, but did not have the desired effect. The first one introduced was "Mr Terry on the piano", which coated with a Yorkshire accent, sounded like "Mr Turry". On saying this the piano still maintained the same rhythm, no big piano solo. The same thing happened as I shouted "Mike on first guitar!"; "Doug on second guitar!"; and "Sam on third!" Again, there was no change in tempo, no difference at all, and when I said "Keg on drums, roll in over one time", no roll came forth, just again the same tempo and on and on. The number finished with a swirl down the piano keyboard, all finishing in unison, and silence! We looked around at each other, big smiles on our happy faces, this had been our first disc. We were delighted with it in spite of the inadequacies.

The B-side was next, a ballad. This was to give some contrast to whoever we might send it, to prove we could be versatile! The number we chose was popular at this time, by Marty Wilde *Why Must I Be A Teenager In Love?* The man disappeared behind the glass again. There was no mad waving this time; thumbs up and we were off. The boys did a smooth harmony introduction to bring me in. This was quite straightforward, plain and simple. Just how plain and simple I discovered on the replay after we had finished. The harmony was excellent, as was the backing. Just one fault, the Yorkshire accent came over, like something from a Brian Rix farce; but it was done and would have to do.

On payment we each received our copy, so from then on we were at least able to boast that a record had been made, as long as the people were not too inquisitive as to the name of the label, as I doubt many people had even heard of Excel Records of Shipley. A funny sequel happened a week later while I was at home. I'd been playing the record on the 'Radiogramme' and while the B-side was playing, the coalman paid his weekly visit for payment. On giving me the change he said in a droll voice "Don't they play some . . . . . rubbish on the radio these days". I blushed and said "Yes, money for old rope." — how could I disagree!

Since forming the group we had played to large and small audiences of all ages, mostly teenagers, but we were not showing any profits — just covering expenses. However, we were becoming quite well known now and people were beginning to call me 'Dal'. We had made a record, and we were enjoying ourselves, so now was the time to chase up bookings, to spread further afield, and to invest in some better equipment. But, alas, all was not happy in the camp. As we suspected, the approaches made earlier by The Dingos for Terry to join them had paid dividends.

So, in the early part of 1960, Terry and the Blue Jays parted company. This meant that the last six months had almost been a waste of time. We would have to start again, but this time, it would be different . . . .

Terry Moran ('Dadio') in his pre-DJ days.
A member of the Blue Jays.

CHAPTER FOUR

If at First
You Don't Succeed ...

Terry leaving to join The Dingos left us in some disarray since most of our numbers were instrumental and the vocals were adapted to include a piano. Anyone can see the problem this set; a complete re-appraisal of the group was required. I still wanted to sing and manage the group, so I had no intention of packing it in. Hopefully my colleagues would be of the same mind, but again I was to be shocked by disillusioned Blue Jays handing in their notice. Within a week of Terry leaving, Doug Lamb, our lead guitarist, decided he had had enough. I believe Doug had set his musical career with a better group and seeing our prospects were not looking good, upped and left. Incidentally, Doug eventually also played with The Dingos, so maybe the Dal Stevens' groups were good for exports to go on to better groups!

As all this was going on I was cancelling bookings, bookings that we had all worked hard for, but what else could I do? No pianist and no lead guitar, panic had set in. The next to succumb was Keg our drummer. To this day I do not know what became of Keg. "Roll it one time Keg".

Next to go was our rhythm guitarist Sam. All this took place within six days, leaving myself and first lieutenant, bass guitarist Mike Farrell. Mike, I knew I could depend on, and he was to be very helpful in the forming of a new group.

We decided, the two of us, to try and reorganise a new group as soon as possible. Mike would try his contacts, I mine.

As I was now the manager of a totally defunct group, my mind was in a turmoil as to where to start. Remember, we required two of the most vital ingredients of a group, a lead guitarist, who were not plentiful since all the good ones were already established with the other groups. The same can also be said of drummers - scarce.

I am sure we could not have gone on with this run of bad luck, and we didn't. Our luck turned. Within a week we had both a lead guitarist, rhythm guitarist and drummer.

The drummer was introduced to me through a mutual friend, who asked him to come and see me at my home at Ruffield Side,

'Dal Stevens' of the Four Dukes at Grattan's Charity Dance, 1960. (LEFT: John Lund; RIGHT: Keith Artist)

Wyke. Keith Artist was the drummer's name. I remember listening to him for the first time and thinking this is what had been lacking previously, with respect to our late drummer Keg. Keith had that professional quality and, although young, just seventeen, he had experience of some two years, from Skiffle to Rock 'n' Roll groups.

The rhythm guitarist who came forward and joined us was John Lund, a colleague who worked , as I did, at Grattan Warehouse. Incidentally, I joined Grattan Warehouse on leaving the army hoping this would be a stopgap of a few months until making the 'Big Time'. That two months turned into nearly three years which, if I had not left, would have turned me into a robot. (I saw other people who had been there a few years acting out scenes like Charlie Chaplin's film *Modern Times* where Charlie is seen working on a production line. His job is to tighten two large nuts with two equally large spanners on a conveyor belt during the course of two second intervals. Hence boredom, repetition, resulting in an almost robot affliction.)

John was a quiet, artistic youth, and quite an accomplished rhythm guitarist, who I felt sure would weld a new bond between all new members.

The acquisition of the lead guitarist cost me 1/6 (7½p) for an advert in the musicians' column in the *Telegraph & Argus*. It read:

> *'Wanted Urgently 'lead guitarist' for established group.*
> *Must have experience - write 47 Ruffield Side, Wyke.'*

Note some of the points in the advert.'Established group' — what group? We were two of a defunct group, a new drummer and a rhythm guitarist who had not even played with us. 'Must have experience' — so this was the 'Bernard Delfont' of Wyke! Note also the address, no 'phone number. Why? because these were the days of the 'phone box and someone-down-the-road-who-had-a-'phone; 'phones were not the luxury we take for granted today.

All my bookings had been made by letter. On reflection I don't know how it worked so well, but it did. Also, I have noticed that on nearly all the local groups' business cards of that period there *were* no 'phone numbers, and I know it was not unusual for some car from a pub or club to call at the group leader's home and ask if they could play that night. Believe me, this happened many times and in most cases completed the requirement. Also, remember that probably no private transport was available, only public transport.

So, the advert appeared. Forgetting that there was a lunchtime edition of the *Telegraph & Argus,* I was surprised when the doorbell rang around 5.15 pm. On opening the door there stood our future hope, Eric

Holroyd. Eric was a good six foot and was dressed in a smart desk suit, string tie and carrying a canvas holder containing his guitar. He said he'd seen my advert that lunchtime and had made his way up from his home which, I seem to remember, had the salubrious name of Gashouse Row, Listerhills. To this day I don't know whether Eric had dressed himself up to meet a top impressario, or if it was his normal attire. As I had to admit, he looked a typical group member, but could he play? Luckily, I had our small amplifier into which Eric plugged his accoustic guitar. He started off by doing a few introductions of popular numbers of the time. Every one was perfect. I sat and watched him make that guitar talk. Eric was just what we needed, but would he join us, especially after my revelations of the so-called group I had advertised? "Yes," was the answer, "no problem". He had just been swanning around different groups and now decided he wanted a permanent position in a permanent group. Well, time would tell.

To reform the group would mean changing the name, as we had left problems when cancelling bookings as the Blue Jays. I kept my name as 'Dal Stevens', but the name changed to The Four Dukes. So it was that Dal Stevens and The Four Dukes were born.

A place of practice was required, and quickly, if we were to establish ourselves on the scene. Storr Hill Baths, Wyke, was our first practice venue. Again, the group had to arrive there from all areas of Bradford — 10 am Sunday mornings.

The Dependable Mike Farrell in his last appearance with the Four Dukes.

The first practice went very well with Eric as lead. He did lead, and the numbers we learnt were quick and different. Come the second Sunday of practice and the local residents of Storr Hill had had enough with Sunday practice No 1. Not again were they to be awakened by the ranting and ravings of an up-and-coming group spoiling their Sunday morning lay-ins after their Saturday booze-ups.

We had set our equipment up and had barely got through Cliff Richard's *Move It* when a deadly missile in the shape of a half-brick came crashing through one of the windows, narrowly missing Keith's head and his prized drum kit. It did not need a second barrage because no group has ever dismantled guitars, amplifiers and drums in this unrecorded record time. We had no transport so, with equipment dangling from running figures, we scurried up Storr Hill to the nearest bus stop to regroup, leaving no equipment behind, just the sound of laughter from many of the Sunday morning sleepers who had put to fright what might have become one of the world's leading groups with one missile. As we nervously huddled around the bus stop, we waited for an out-of-control mob to tear us and our equipment to pieces, but no-one came, and everything again was still and tranquil as the people of Storr Hill went back to sleep. We were now left with the dilemma of finding somewhere safe to practice.

A quick advert in the Telegraph followed — *'Rock 'n' Roll group require place to practice"*. I had not long to wait. The response was from the caretaker of Unity Hall, Rawson Square. They had a spare room we could use for 10/- (50p) a week.

So I booked our new place of practice for four weeks. I cannot emphasise enough what a problem it was to make sure we all turned up on the night of the practice. It was not worrying about some of the group not turning up, but the conveyance of the equipment. Keith's was the worst problem - his drum kit. Luckily Keith's father had a small Ford Prefect and most times he would run Keith with his drum kit, from his house in Bankfoot to the venue or practice, and pick him up. The name 'group' means 'group', and while you could practice without the odd guitarist, it was quite useless to try practice without a drummer. So we were reliant on the good nature of Keith's father.

But there were times when his father could not transport him, and Keith, being the person he was, would endeavour to get his drum kit on an ordinary transport bus. His kit was in large bakerlite cases with straps, with the large drum, snare drum, top hat cymbal, two foot sticks, etc. He would struggle to Bankfoot to try and catch the Huddersfield to Bradford bus which was the normal Bradford City bus. This had a larger storage compartment than the old red Hebble buses, so, with ease, he could transport his equipment in the City bus. But if a small pushchair was already placed under the stairs, then he'd had it, await the next, and try again. The buses used to unload their passengers at the side of the Town Hall, just before Dalby's Antiques on the left hand side. With all this equipment Keith would have to struggle across to the front of Town Hall Square, around the front of the Mechanics Institute, up Ivegate, turn right along Kirkgate, passing H. Samuel's, Burton's, Kirkgate Market, turn left up Darley Street, left at the top, and into Rawson Square, and to Unity Hall. All this to practice! Hard to believe, but true. On two occasions while we were practicing at Unity Hall, Keith had no transport, and this is what he did. The return journey was the same, only he had some help from myself.

It was on the second occasion that I was helping on the return journey that we walked into the cameras of *Room at the Top*. They were filming a scene by 'The Boy and Barrel' entrance, which was supposedly the entrance to a theatre on which part of the film was based. We stood for a while and watched, and saw Lawrence Harvey and Simone Signoret. But we were then asked to moved on as we looked like part of the film crew with all these objects wrapped around us. *Room at the Top* — was that an omen? We shrugged, re-adjusted our weights, and continued down Ivegate into the gloomy night for our bus home.

Our first booking as Dal Stevens and The Four Dukes was a special charity concert held by Grattan at the village hall in Clayton. We were on the bill with a variety of other artistes made up of people who worked at Grattan. It was a nervous time again, but we had practiced hard. We had some good numbers and we went down quite well, that being the general reaction of seeing the audience again when back at Grattan the next morning.

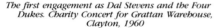

SOME SMART STEPPING by THE LOREEN BUNN TROUPE

THE SHOWMEN TAKE THE STAGE

THE RELIEF OF RHUBARB ... ... COLIN and IRENE

OUR DANCE STYLIST ... ... OLYWEN WORBY

MEMORIES OF A STAR, No. 2. - - - THE OLD MAN
        with ERIC, CLIFF, KEN and LINDA

OUR GUEST ARTISTE
Dal Stevens and the Four Dukes

SHORT SKETCH ... ... CONVERSATION PIECE

JOIN US IN AN
Old Tyme Music Hall
Your Chairman HUGH introduces
THE SINGING WAITERS
WOLSEY and FORD ... ... THE LOREEN BUNN TROUPE
and THE COMPANY

THE QUEEN

The first engagement as Dal Stevens and the Four Dukes. Charity Concert for Grattan Warehouse, Clayton, 1960

'Duane': the new bass guitarist of the Four Dukes (aged 16).

At the same time, Mike Farrell, who had stuck with me from the beginning, decided to call it a day and, as we knew someone who worked at Grattan and wished to join a group as a bass guitarist, Mike knew he would not be causing us problems, so he left feeling not guilty. We were all sorry to see him go because, unlike most people, Mike was liked by everyone, so I knew I had a void to fill both in a likeable person and good guitarist. But for once I had no need to worry because we had Dennis 'Duane' Oliver, aged sixteen, to join us. Duane had no problem in fitting in and soon familiarised himself with our numbers. A plus for Duane was that he could sing like Cliff Richard. This was indeed a bonus. In fact, Duane had a much better voice than mine, and I look back and think that if I had not been manager as well as vocalist, I could have been out of a job. His only problem, which he soon overcame, was his nervousness. Being only sixteen, and coming straight into a group, nearly all of whom had some experience, could be unnerving. But Duane soon became one of the more professional and polished members of the group. So, I now had the group, what now?

CHAPTER FIVE

Snakes and Ladders

We were soon back on the same circuit for bookings. The Majestic ballroom on Mondays, The Gaumont ballroom on Sundays; these were both Rock 'n' Roll nights. Also regularly at The Students' Club. The Students' Club gave low pay but had great atmosphere. Anyone who was anyone played at that club. It was situated at the end of New Victoria Street, or Prince's Way, under the newsagents on the corner, just near the Alassio Coffee Bar. The entrance was a small single door leading down some steps into a large open cellar in which there were large ornate Victorian pillars holding up the wooden floor above. At one end was a two-foot high platform. This was the stage, and was about ten foot across by eight foot deep. In front of this so-called stage were a few rows of wooden benches. Behind this, people who did not wish to sit, could stand. At the back was a counter where soft drinks were sold, and somewhere to the rear were the toilets. The lighting was somewhat subdued due to the lack of sockets; this being a Victorian building. The establishment was run by a bearded gentleman called Michael who, with his wife, ran a very well organised and popular 'scene' of that era, liking it to The Cavern in Liverpool, (although our particular students' club, and atmosphere, was well established before the so-called Cavern!).

You had to be a member, but not necessarily a student. Members could also take in guests, so the number was unlimited. For 'passouts' your hand was stamped with a colour dye which was very hard to forge, so this caused no problems. In the bowels of Bradford, and looking like something out of Oliver Twist, air was required. This was also part of the atmosphere. The windows, which were high up in the cellar, opened partly on ground level with the pavement outside the newsagents. So, with these windows open, the music sailed into the evening for the passers by to love or ridicule, while the really young people could only wish for the time when *they* would be able to go down below. (Although it must be said that there were thirteen to fourteen year olds down there. But at least they would not be in an alcoholic atmosphere, there being no alcohol licence.) Generally there were three groups on and, again, we were with The Mel Clarke Four and topping the bill, The Cresters.

As previously stated, the pay was low, but just to play there was pay enough. I've been told that David Hockney did a large mural on one of the walls in The Students' Club. If so, when this area was pulled down in the mid-Sixties, what happened to it? Is it still down there waiting for future archaeologists to discover? An original 20th Century David Hockney mural!

One of the unusual bookings to get in this period was one at a picture house during the film interval. It never did catch on; since the patrons had already paid to see the film, why pay extra for a group to entertain? Our one and only booking of this kind came from the Low Moor picture house, affectionately known as the 'Grott', 'Grotty' or 'Grotto'. Take your pick, all were appropriate! The stage area from the front to the big silver screen was approximately four foot. Try placing five male adults, three amplifiers, and a large set of drums in this area! To do this the drums had to go partly offstage so, once in position, we could not move backwards or forwards. We must have looked like five dummies in a Burton's shop window. Needless to say, we did not need that kind of booking again. It was a memorable night though because Eric could not make it and asked a friend of his, Sammy King, a brilliant guitarist and song writer, to help out, which he did.

LIKE CRAZY, MAN!!
At the Students' Club, Tomorrow, 8.0.
THE MEL CLARKE FOUR.
DAL and THE FOUR DUKES.
MICK SAGAR
and THE CRESTAS

MEMBER'S

CARD

1960—61

THE STUDENTS' CLUB
(Proprietors: P. J. P. Dennehy Ltd.)
6 NEW VICTORIA STREET · BRADFORD 1
Tel. Bradford 28002

MEMBERSHIP   No   1553

ABOVE (TOP): Students' Club advert in the Telegraph & Argus. ABOVE (CENTRE & BOTTOM): Membership Card for the Students' Club. (The membership number indicates just how popular the club was).
BELOW: Victoria Square, 1965. The Students' Club was situated on the corner. Its entrance was by the belisha beacon. (Courtesy Bradford Libraries and Information Service).

ABOVE: The Low Moor Picture Palace, affectionately known as the "Grott" (Photo: R.E. Preedy, 1983).
Courtesy C. J. Mellor, *The Cinemas of Bradford.*

BELOW: SAMMY KING. Brilliant guitarist and song writer helped out Dal and his Four Dukes at the salubrious Low Moor Picture Palace.

While the surroundings were not as we could wish, the help and professionalism from Sammy did rub off. Incidentally, Sammy wrote the hit number for Roy Orbison called *Penny Arcade.*

So, from the ridiculous to the sublime, namely the Gaumont cinema (now Odeon), Bradford. Between 1950 and 1965 The Gaumont cinema staged many shows, but the difference for our booking was an event called the *Teenage Show* on Saturday mornings. It was the idea of the then manager, Mr Philcox, who knew of us playing at the Gaumont Ballroom and Majestic. His idea was to have a teenage show consisting of two groups between 10 am and 12 noon, where youngsters could dance at the front of the stage, or even come onto the stage and dance. This could sound ridiculous, but it wasn't, because of the sheer size of the stage - 70' wide by 45' deep. We were lost on a stage of that size, so much so that a false back drop was brought down to narrow this. I had never thought I would appear on this stage.

In 1945 I had joined the Gaumont Saturday Morning Club, consisting of a sing-along — the one with the bouncing ball moving over

Dal Stevens and the Four Dukes on stage for the Gaumont Theatre's Saturday Morning Teenage Show. (LEFT TO RIGHT: Eric, Keith, Duane, John, Dal and Mr. Philcox, the manager.)

GAUMONT THEATRE
BRADFORD TEL. 26716

HEY TEENAGERS! DIG THIS!
YOUR OWN SHOW!

THE TEENAGE SHOW

AT 10 A.M. (DOORS OPEN 9.30 A.M.)

ADMISSION 1/-

FILMS! JIVE SESSIONS! ACTS!
STARTS
SATURDAY, 21st MAY

- GROUPS -
- VOCALISTS -
- INSTRUMENTALISTS -
WANTED IMMEDIATELY

Apply by letter for audition to:-
THE MANAGER
GAUMONT THEATRE
BRADFORD
BY APRIL 9th LATEST

An invitation to audition.

PHIL RIDLER, Manager of the New Victoria (later Gaumont) from its opening in 1930 until his retirement in 1957. Known affectionately to the many thousands of youngsters who attended the Saturday Morning Club as Uncle Phil.

the words on the screen. This was accompanied by the giant Wurlitzer organ which had previously arisen from the depths of the cinema. After the songs, Uncle Phil (Ridler), the manager, would find his way down from the top of the stalls to a microphone on the stage. All the way down he would be dodging the many missiles that were aimed at him from all corners. This was also accompanied by a loud booing and stamping of feet. Arriving at the microphone he would give us a little message, though no-one could hear it. Then we sang the National Anthem, followed by a cartoon, serial, and picture.

A few years later, in my Disc Jockey capacity, I met Mr Ridler (Uncle Phil) and asked him "Why the National Anthem *before* the films?", to which his logical answer was "Did you wait to the very end of the picture?". Looking back, nearly everyone seemed to be edging up the aisles to the doors to rush out while still watching the film. You were not allowed to sit in the back stalls, only the front stalls. The only time this did not apply was after the 1946 flood. The Gaumont had been under water, just like the rest of Bradford, but it had only affected the lower front stalls. The back stalls, being at a higher level, had not been hit. For weeks after you could see the tide mark where the water had reached.

Now, some fourteen years later, I was to be on that same stage for the Teenage Show. Hopefully we might draw a crowd, but with 3,300 seats to fill, it was not likely, and we knew it. We were right of course. We played there three times on the Saturday mornings, but it did not really take off as there were only a hundred to two hundred people each time, and these were mostly the very young, youngsters whose mothers had probably pushed them in to get rid of them for a couple of hours while they went shopping. But we did gain the experience of playing in a marvellous theatre with excellent acoustics. You can see from the photograph how lost we looked, Mr Philcox had just thanked us — I remember he called me Dale Stevens. Our pay was four guineas, so it paid expenses, and got us known just that little bit more.

Mr Philcox, another of nature's fine gentlemen, knew we were having problems finding a place to practice. Our struggles to Unity Hall and the additional expense it was costing finally proved too much and Mr Philcox, hearing of our predicament, offered us one of the ten dressing rooms to practice on Wednesday evenings. This was not only very convenient, but was not to cost us a penny. It meant that, playing mostly in the centre of Bradford, Keith could leave his drum kit, which could be safely locked up, thus saving all our previous problems regarding forthcoming bookings. When I received an answer that we had a booking, I had to write to Eric as he was the only one I could not contact directly. John, Duane and I worked at Grattan, and Keith could be contacted quite easily at his place of work. But a letter had to go to Eric's home in Listerhills. A return letter came back from Eric, for during a Saturday morning Teenage Show his trumpet was stolen. Yes, trumpet! Although an excellent guitarist, he also wished to play the trumpet, so he had brought it down to leave in the rehearsal room, to have the odd practice when we had our rehearsal sessions on Wednesday evenings. He said he thought it might have been one of us who took it as he knew we were not too keen on him wanting to introduce a trumpet into an odd number. We swore to Eric that none of us had touched his trumpet. Eric's trumpet has never been seen since.

Our practice room was on the first floor balcony of the theatre of which the entrance was through the balcony, down the side, through the double doors. So many times we had to proceed through while the film was on, causing remarks from some of the teenage girls who, in the darkness, could distinguish the guitars being carried. This became ridiculous because, in the end, we started showing off, sometimes coming through when the lights had gone up during an intermission knowing that these young females would be saying "Who is it?", "What group are you?" This is when the lies began to stream forth. Yes, we have been on TV. Yes, we have just been on a tour with Gene Vincent, and so on. Many locals knew who we were so there was no kidding them, but it had to stop after one of our jokes backfired.

One week we knew that Cliff Richard and The Shadows were due to play at the theatre on Saturday. On the Wednesday we decided we would enter the balcony when it was really dark and rush down the

Inside the Gaumont Theatre showing the first floor balcony (right hand side) entrance to our practice sessions where our Cliff Richard saga took place. Photo: J.Scwires. Courtesy G. J. Mellor, The Cinemas of Bradford.

side towards our dressing room. Eric was to be our main prop as he was tall and, with dark glasses on, he looked like Hank Marvin, Cliff's lead guitarist. As we others did not seem to resemble any of the other Shadows we would make most noise shouting remarks like "Come on Hank, hurry or you will be seen", etc. Most people knew that Cliff and The Shadows were due to appear that weekend.

It did not take much hinting, going down those balcony steps on the Wednesday evening, that the Shadows had arrived, plus Cliff Richard. Looking back, what touring group would arrive three days early? No-one queried that. Word was buzzing through the theatre. With shouts to Hank, we were through the balcony doors and into the passage leading to our first floor dressing room. The drums already being in position, we soon had the guitars ready. As I said previously, Duane could sing like Cliff Richard. The windows of the dressing room looked down on to the bottom of Morley Street, facing the Alhambra. As on other nights of practice we knew the sound would sail into the still night air. The dressing rooms were sound proofed, so none of our playing could be heard in the theatre, but this did not stop a crowd of young teenagers, who had supposedly come to watch a film, congregate around the balcony door leading to the dressing room. The cinema usherettes could see something was amiss and were soon on the spot asking the many girls to please return to their seats. All this while the very large screen was lit up with the film of the week. "Cliff Richard had not arrived", they were told, "But we've seen him!" was the reply. "And Hank", another said. As I was in the dressing room I did not know all this was going on, but I was told by one of the usherettes later. She had said that when Mr Philcox had been called he had considered putting the house lights on to sort the situation out. After playing Cliff Richard's *Please don't Touch* twice we were about to play *Apache* when Mr Philcox arrived in the dressing room to inform us that, during our entry for our practice, we had been mistaken for Cliff Richard. We all looked at each other in amazement! How could anyone mistake Dal Stevens and The Four Dukes for such a star group? Mr Philcox was as much surprised as we ourselves were.

But while we were discussing the situation a chant was coming through the windows and, on looking out, we could see that quite a crowd had gathered. They were chanting "We want Cliff". Word had filtered out-side and with the sound of Cliff's number coming from the window people had really believed that he was in the building. Every time we showed a head at the window screams and shouts generated through the air. With this, Mr Philcox said we should not play any more numbers and close the window. This we did and sat around waiting for the noise to subside.

We had entered that building to practice at 7.30 pm and had to wait there until after 11.00 pm before we could leave. This was because we had to wait until the film ended, as we had to go out the way we came in, and with rumours being rife, it might have started up again. I do not believe we pulled the wool over Mr Philcox's eyes, even though we tried to act innocently. I think he knew all this had developed out of nothing. The last buses had gone, out-side was again still and quiet, and what did Mr Philcox do? He paid for two taxis to take us home.

CHAPTER SIX

Bradford's Other Pleasures

Bradford still had other pursuits in the late Fifties and, early Sixties for the teenagers to follow. Hardly anything had changed since before the war. Kirkgate Market and the Swan Arcade were still present in all their Victorian glory. So was the open air market with its pie and pea stalls and a special soap stall which sold a soap (Sloamans) especially for spots, so doing a roaring trade with us all. Bradford City Football Club was going through a good period having players like McCole, John Read, Derek Stokes and Jim Lawler. They were doing well in both league and cup matches, drawing crowds of over 10,000 who were looked after by about six policemen. Every night the *Telegraph & Argus* would show under entertainments some thirty-six picture houses in and around Bradford. So, if not dancing, most went to the pictures twice a week.

Bradford's Open-air Market, Westgate, where Sloaman's Soap did a roaring trade with the juvenile 'Spot' brigade. 'Big Anna' was often seen helping out on some of the stalls. (Courtesy: Mrs M Bruce, Bradford Photographic Survey and Bradford Libraries and Information Service)

Television had still not reached all areas and only had two channels: BBC TV and ITV, of which the latter had not been established long. Both channels showed programmes from 5.00 pm until 11.45 pm and then closedown. Not much in the way of Rock 'n' Roll was shown so we had to be content with the odd topping of the bill on *Sunday Night at the London Palladium* for some of our stars. Other programmes to watch were *Dig This, Six-Five Special* and *Juke Box Jury,* and all this in black and white, and where the average television screen was only twelve inches. Radio (wireless) had BBC Light and Home (North) Services. Only two programmes seemed to stand out, *Pick of the Pops* on Saturday nights and Jack Jackson's *Record Roundup.* But by far the most popular was Radio Luxembourg's *Top Twenty* on a Sunday night from 11.00 pm until 12.00 am. This brought you up to date with all the top numbers - the ones you liked.

A variation of the TWIST at the Textile Hall, 1963. (Note the special dancing boots on the young lady on the right).

Tyrrel Street, 1966. In this block were Farmer Giles' Cafe, The Empress Hotel, and, above Burton's, the Gaiety Ballroom.

Courtesy of Bradford Photographic Survey (Mrs. M Bruce) and Bradford Libraries and Information Service.

The modern ballroom dancer was well catered for with the Gaiety on Tyrrell Street. Almost every night music from this dance hall above Burton's would filter through the windows down into the street, letting everyone hear of the good things happening above. Textile Hall and the Milton Rooms, both in Westgate, had their regular attenders, but the more refined kept clear and attended the more assured setting of the Majestic with Billy Hey's Orchestra and the Gaumont Ballroom with Bert Bentley's. The Kings and Queens, Morley Street, were popular, but were more for special events like staff dances and student balls.

QUEEN'S HALL.
VIEW LOOKING TOWARDS KING'S HALL.

When the King's Hall was required for dancing a sprung floor was placed over the pool. Few people realised what waited below as hundreds of feet pounded the boards!
(Source: Souvenir booklet on the *Re-Opening of the Windsor Halls*. City of Bradford, 1919.)

Having no regular weekday dances, Bert Shutts at Bankfoot had always been popular, but had got rather bad publicity because of a large fight that had taken place outside one night when Teddy Boys and others had been using flick knives, causing casualties in a running fight around Bankfoot. Again, in outer areas, the small Kings and Queens at Idle were still good outlets, as was the Somerset at Undercliffe, and moving out to Shipley, the Lakean Ballroom. Back in the centre of Bradford, the Co-op Hall off Thornton Road, again a lovely ballroom, had its Saturday night dances, thus making, within a small radius of a few hundred yards, six or more dance halls. Admission charges varied from 1/6 (7½p) to 7/6 (37½p) and even 10/- (50p), and for that price it had to be something special. Of course, not everyone was keen on Rock 'n' Roll and there were many jazz clubs around with both traditional and modern. The Wool City Jazzmen were very popular, playing many times at the Market Tavern on the top side of Kirkgate Market. Transport services to all these venues were excellent, both from the diesel and trolley buses. As most of these services finished around 11.00 pm, people could be seen scurrying around Bradford centre every evening as the Town Hall was gearing itself up to give us its 11 o'clock chimes. From many shop and warehouse doorways courting couples would emerge to get that last bus, leaving, in many cases, the males to walk home, especially if their last bus was at the other side of Bradford. But this was the accepted thing.

In this area were six dance halls within a few hundred yards of each other: Gaumont, Majestic, King's Hall, Queen's Hall, Co-op Hall and the Gaiety, plus the Students' Club.
(Courtesy Bradford Libraries and Information Service)

So, after 11 o'clock, Bradford would take on the look of a ghost town. Traffic would diminish and things would come to a standstill. You might be lucky and have some money for a taxi and could go join the queue in Town Hall Square where the price was about 3/- (15p) to all outlying districts, or, if you weren't so lucky, you could begin the long walk home. Females as well as males took these walks after missing buses, either in groups or singles, and it seems in doing so hardly any trouble occured. The most that people had to contend with on these treks was the occasional drunk, for whom you merely crossed over to the other side of the road, thus avoiding trouble. Of course, some dances did run late and those without cars had the option of walking or late night buses. These were Corporation buses hired by the organisation whose dance it was. So if some company were running a staff dance these late buses would be laid on. You paid around 1/6 (7½p) for this service. On paying, the conductor would make a list out of the areas and proceed on a round trip of Bradford. If lucky your area might be one of the first visited. Night Clubs were non-existent, so if you did wish to prolong your stay after 11.00 pm the most probable place to go was a Chinese restaurant. One of these that was available at the time was The Dragon and Peacock which used to be Laycock's Restaurant. This was down Albion Court, the passage off Kirkgate and was very popular, if not very decorative. If you were lucky to live in the Carlisle Road area, then there was Pie-Toms where meat pies, mushy peas and mint sauce at 1/6 (7½p) could finish the night off nicely. Another Chinese Restaurant in those early days was at Bankfoot terminus, although this place had a reputation of Chinese waiters chasing people with hatchets who forgot to pay their bill. Other than those mentioned, eating out was limited and was not in great demand like it is today.

Law and order was subject to the old Bradford City Police Force, most of whom were local men and thus knew the area and local villains. The police were still respected and, in most cases, a word was sufficient to stop any trouble. Of course, there were occasions when teenagers *were* rebellious so there were times when actions did speak louder than words! With everybody working the next day, people had to get those last buses. If you were wandering around the centre of Bradford after 1.00 am you were most likely up to no good. One of the popular meeting places was the Alex. It was then the Alexander Hotel, formerly the Old Empire Theatre. Being situated up Great Horton Road, it was very central, and most nights found it well attended with students and workers alike, having the odd drink before going to a dance, the pictures or theatre. At the bottom of Manchester Road, on the corner, was the Majestic pub, again very central. The most popular bar in this establishment was downstairs, known as Viv's Bar. It was small but cosy. This was the place where you always found someone you knew. The old Talbot Hotel in Kirkgate, with the statue of the dog above the door, still boasted a gentleman's bar where attending females were frowned upon. There were always the pubs of notoriety that older people would tell you not to go in, notably The New Inn off Town Hall Square. Up Ivegate The Kings Head and The Grosvenor were ones to be warned of. Also, on Tyrell Street, The Old Back Empress Hotel had a certain calling. A few doors away poor old Farmer Giles' Milk Bar had a certain reputation that it could not shake off. Further along Broadway was the Old Iron Gates. I once called in to be greeted by a scene from Dickens, full of street newspaper vendors, wooden legs and eye patches. It was like being in a time warp of 1860, not 1960. Old Kate Kennedy, one of the few Bradford characters, was coming to the end of her reign. She could still be seen wandering around the Manchester Road area, and she would be most likely chalking up another appearance in court for being drunk and disorderly, her many appearances totalling hundreds.

Another character of a more orderly disposition was Anna, affectionately known to most as 'Big Anna', who frequented the open air market, helping the stallholders distribute their goods. She could hold three tins of peas in her hands. Asking "Who would like a tin of peas?", nobody would dare refuse.

The Majestic Pub at the bottom of Manchester Road, Viv's Bar was situated downstairs. (Source: Bradford Libraries and Information Service).

Yet another character who has survived from the early Sixties to the present day is Judas, Jesus or the Monk. A bearded fresh-looking gentleman wearing brown sackcloth and open sandals. For years he has been wandering our city streets waving at vehicles and greeting pedestrians with a hearty "Good Morning". In the early Sixties the response to his politeness was "Swinging" (Norman Vaughan of the London Palladium's catchy phrase of the time). Why and what he has been preaching or trying to achieve all these years has baffled the public, but at least he is consistant. Although I do know one thing for sure, he has his trousers rolled up under his garb!

Fashion was well catered for, especially if you wished for "with it" gear. For the males, Hargreaves outfitters up Sunbridge Road had a nice selection of frilled-type shirts, string ties and the popular luminous socks (lime green), as did Wallis outfitters at the bottom of Manchester Road, who also could offer all the trendy wear and were not as expensive as Hargreaves. Casual wear and flower power was not to show itself until the mid-Sixties, so most males wore a suit or jacket of some kind, plus a shorty raincoat which was taking the place of the large gaberdine raincoat which everybody seemed to carry over the arm, even when it was not raining.

Hairstyles for the males were conjured up from the local barbers who were plentiful, but perhaps the favourite for your 'Tony Curtis' or 'DA' style was Mario's in Forster Square, who had something to offer rather than the usual back-and-sides favoured by our fathers. On the female side, fashion was dominated by skirts, with many underskirts giving a stand-out effect, high heels, and many changes of hairstyle from the Pixie and Beehive to the Bouffant.

Not many young people had a car. For most the only ride in a car would be a taxi to the station (en route to holidays). Those who could not quite afford a car went for the popular Vespa or Lambrettas which abounded, or if you wished to show off, a bubble car, a four-wheeled contraption with a large door at the front which opened up to climb into. A less popular mode of transport, but very effective for getting around, was the Messerschmitt. This was half the size of a bubble car and shaped like an aeroplane cockpit. The top would open up to a front single seat and one at the rear, so with two people it was like being in an aircraft. Even the steering wheel was shaped like an aircraft control column.

You had to have some money for this, or any other mode of transport, and money depended on your job. At that time most of the mills were still operational, thus giving plenty of jobs for both males and females, either in office work at the mill, or in the mill itself as Liggers, Doffers, Combers, Spinners, etc. Also, plenty of office work was available in Bradford for typists or clerical staff. Apprenticeships had to be served for mechanics, engineers and electricians. Large companies like English Electric and Croft Engineering were prominent in the area for young people. If none of these was fancied, then there was always shopwork from the large stores like Brown Muffs, the Co-op, and Busby's, to the small corner shops.

Kate Kennedy's 'Wandering Ground' at the bottom of Manchester Road. (About 1970). Demolition in progress. Wallis outfitters has just disappeared.
(Courtesy Bradford Libraries and Information Service.)

Wages around this period varied from £8.00 to £12.00 per week and, if you were lucky, some overtime could add an extra 10/- (50p) or £1.00 to your wage packet. So the young ones were limited with the amounts to spend. Probably top of the list would be records at around 2/- (10p) for a single. These could be bought at Shackleton's, up Darley Street, or Woods, down Sunbridge Road, who had, until this period, been using booths which you entered and heard the record of your choice through a speaker on the wall of the booth, and then you made up your mind whether you wished to purchase.

Holidays were still spent in England and at special dates that had not been changed for years, like Bank Holiday and Bowling Tide, when most industries closed for a period of time so that its workers could take themselves off to Blackpool or Scarborough for the week, for around £8.00 per week full board.

Last, and probably most popular as a meeting place, were the coffee bars with their frothy coffee. The two most popular of this period were the Alassio in New Victoria Street, a few doors from The Students'

Club, and The Olympus, a few doors from Seabrook's Fisheries up Great Horton Road. Both were renowned and well patronised, owned and run by Cypriots who had a flair for this kind of business. Frothy coffee was the main request, although soft drinks and sandwiches were available. So with a mixture of students and workers, they would spend hours sat with the same coffee planning the next foray or what was the latest news on so-and-so. This, then, was the alternative of the late Fifties and Sixties in Bradford for the teenagers, and while all this was going on, Dal Stevens and The Four Dukes were playing in Bradford as another alternative.

Godwin Street (1975). Further to the left, off Thornton Road, is Southgate and Southgate Hall (Co-op Hall). At the top of Godwin Street on the left is the Co-op Emporium, now Sunwin House.
(Courtesy Bradford Libraries and Information Service.)

CHAPTER SEVEN
As One Door Closes, Another!

Back on the circuits Dal Stevens and The Four Dukes were just about surviving. Bookings were adequate but not well paid. One venue we accepted was a dance ballroom in Selby called Christie's. For a period of one and a half hours we would be paid six guineas. Taking into consideration the hire of a Dormobile - four guineas - it would not leave much to share out between five people. Luckily the van we hired was from another one of Grattan's many employees who would pick up each of us from our locality.

My first and last guitar (Rosetti). Later I would mime the act of playing on stage while Duane sang. This fooled no-one!

DAL   STEVENS

AND THE

FABULOUS

FOUR   DUKES.

ROCK 'N RHYTHM GROUP.

47, Ruffield Side,
Delf Hill,
Wyke, Bradford.

First business card as the Four Dukes. No telephone, but 'Fabulous'!

The booking was for a Saturday night. We had to be there before 7.00 pm in order to set up the equipment and arrange our one and a half hour spot. We had no problem getting there. We were all collected from our respective homes and a pleasant journey ensued. Duane had adorned a large roll of paper with the words 'Dal Stevens and The Four Dukes' in huge red letters. This he fixed around the rear window of the Dormobile, hopefully to cause the many females awaiting our arrival to linger, point, and swoon, or so we hoped. Reaching our destination, we proceeded to unpack the equipment and placed it by the side of the enormous stage. A doorman on duty had directed us in. When the owner/manager appeared, a Mr Blythe, he enquired who we were and when I informed him he retorted that we were booked, but on the 2nd of the following month. As he was making this statement another Dormobile arrived, sporting professionally written slogans advertising the name of the group entombed within. The other group clambered from the van, asked what was happening, and joined in the confrontation. The outcome was that the manager said he would allow us one half hour spot (unpaid) as it was his fault, proved by the fact that I had the letter with me confirming that we were booked for that night. There was no way that we would play for nothing. We loitered a while putting forward our point of view, but to no avail. The other group had the edge. They had played there before and were also on first name terms with Mr Blythe. Today we would have had a solicitor's letter sent, but in those days we hadn't the experience, money or backing of our adversaries. Therefore, with tails between our legs, we trundled back to the van, packed up our equipment and raced off into the night. On the way home Duane disclosed some news that made us all feel better. While the confrontation had been at its height, Duane had mingled with the opposition's equipment, specifically the amplifiers. The result, I heard later, was that the group could not play because of 'faulty' equipment. I can see the group now with their supercilious and superior attitude having to eat humble pie and make their apologies. I look back on Duane's little sortie of that night with relish. This particular group were from South Yorkshire and later appeared on the television. Professionally they were very good, but we had the edge on them at Christie's! Some people have long memories so I won't name the group. I wouldn't like Duane to spend the rest of his life looking over his shoulder. So, when I say we were surviving, I mean it. Fortunately, we were only £2.00 out of pocket as our van driver, being aware of our plight, only charged us this amount, making him no profit at all.

At least with a ballroom, it has its own PA system, whereas one venue we encountered had none. That was the Burley-in-Wharfedale Social Club. Again, with our varied equipment, we had to improvise by using our microphone through one of our amplifiers, to which the rhythm guitar was also connected. Believe me, it doesn't really work, proving another unsuccessful night.

I remember the greeting from the Club Secretary on our arrival "Are you t' band?". "Yes", I said, pointing to the many invisible trumpets, trombones and basoons that we carried. It was not his fault but at that time groups preferred to be called 'groups' as a 'band' meant just that. He said in his letter to me that they were thinking of hiring us on a permanent basis, every Saturday, if we were any good.

There was no stage, so we were squashed in between two billiard tables with about twenty people sitting around the perimeter. With the subdued lighting, heavy smoking, and clinking of glasses I doubt a good night was had by all — including us. Needless to say, we were not invited back, but, one good point, we were paid £6.00.

Variation abounded. Dewsbury Town Hall is well remembered by Dal and his Four Dukes. It was yet another Saturday night and the Ballroom was heaving with over a thousand sweaty bodies gyrating round the floor. The stage was unusual in that it was an island situated near the centre of the dance floor. We had been booked for two half hour spots. The first had been received quite amicably, but it was the second that is impressed on my memory. The phrase 'The band played on' was so appropriate for that evening. I was singing Johnny Kidd's *Shaking All Over* when half way through the number Eric gave me a dig with his guitar and motioned to the extreme rear of the ballroom where a fight had begun.

We had seen the odd skirmish before in other places. These were generally put down almost immediately by the dinner-suited bouncers employed for situations such as this. However, on this occasion the fracas spread like wildfire in what seemed seconds. From two to three people having a go it was now two to three hundred. A huge wave of people, arms and legs flying, surged around our island — where the band played on. At one point the Gents toilet door was flung open and inside we glimpsed bloody heads making contact with white tiles. No-one suggested we play on, in fact, no-one could have got near us to relay such a message, but we did just that. Fear, I think, encouraged us to continue.

Not one attempt was made to climb up onto the island. If we had stopped we would have been engulfed in a matter of seconds and our equipment destroyed and ourselves also. This all took place within five minutes at which point a massive contingent of Police arrived. People were pulled outside onto the pavement and gradually subdued.

At that point a small number of people started to dance again until the scene became as if nothing had happened. During this time we had not dared to change the number. We reckoned we had completed *Shaking all over* five times over. The Police informed the management that, as we had continued to play the music, it acted as another distraction and, had we stopped, one hundred per cent attention would have been given to the fight, resulting in even more people taking part. We were rewarded by being given an extra £1.00 each. That night was the most we were to earn (£15.00 between five).

In between the bookings and my work at Grattan some time had to be made to obtain bookings. Some came through Mr Lawrance, obtaining bookings both at the Majestic and Gaumont. Others from the many letters I wrote.

Before the advent of Yorkshire Television , Yorkshire was served by Granada Television from Manchester. On many teatime occasions Mike Scott or Bill Grundy (well known at that time) would introduce up-and-coming groups. Being the manager of that type of group, I wrote to Bill Grundy asking to be considered for a spot on *Granada In the North*. But we were one of many unsuccessful hopefuls. So, what next?

The Mecca, Leeds, was drawing large crowds, especially with a new local type of DJ who was also making a name for himself on the radio. For once I did not write, but telephoned from a call box. With a little luck and plenty of cheek I finally got through to him. He listened politely to what I had to say then explained that just like Granada he, too, was overwhelmed with groups wanting a booking. Unless we were something special then we were just one of many also-rans. Jimmy advised more experience etc, etc, and something different. Yes, Jimmy — Jimmy Saville!

Looking back the advice was sound. What most groups required in those days were the entrepreneurs like Brian Epstein: someone to encourage, organise, and financially back them. I'm not saying we would have been a great success if we had been fortunate enough to have had the backing but, like ourselves, most of the local groups at that time were their own organisers/managers and without capital. I am sure that if Bradford had been more organised, with people to back local groups, then the Bradford scene may have developed long before the Mersey sound was ever heard of.

At this point we were treading water. Eric was beginning to get agitated and, being married, wanted extra money. Offers from other groups were being received by Duane because of his singing voice - so much like Cliff Richard. Keith, I think, needed to be more successful. Only John and myself seemed content until things could get better. As it happened something helped us make the decision.

As in most groups, some of the members had girlfriends who, as a rule, we kept separate from the group. By that, I mean we did not allow them to accompany us to any venues. The reasons were, firstly, the extra time needed picking up and taking home, and secondly, the female sat about (probably on her own) in a strange place while the boyfriend was playing and wondering if she was OK, or looking from the stage and wondering who that bloke was chatting her up. With respect to the females, when they get together in this situation, the group does not behave as a group any more: there are too many diversions. After some time this rule became lax and the odd one or two group members brought their girlfriends along. This came to a head one night when we were returning from a booking. We dropped one of the group off and said we would drop his girlfriend off at her address which was the other side of town. This was done, no problem, until the next day when that member of the group accused another member of chatting up his girlfriend on the way home after he had been dropped off. There was no truth in this, but it caused so much animosity that within a week Dal Stevens and the Four Dukes were no more. So, after many trials and tribulations, and many reasons which could have caused us to disband, it required something so simple to push us over the edge. If we had been in a stronger, more successful position, we would have probably survived. As it was we just needed a little push.

CHAPTER EIGHT

Star of Another Kind

W hat does one do after two years of being in a group? For myself, I was disappointed as I had enjoyed being in the public eye. I had only a week to wait for opportunity to knock once more and put me back into the limelight.

The Gaumont Ballroom had been having its Sunday 'Big Beat' night for some months and had only recently started to attract live pop stars on stage in the ballroom. The first one was Jess Conrad; admission was 4/6 (22½p). This would be augmented by a local group like ourselves. Knowing most of the local groups, I decided to go and see what it was like on the outside looking in. While at the bar (soft drinks only) the manager came up to have a word, his name was Ray Moore. Ray had worked at Grattan where I had known

Ray Moore, Manager, Gaumont Ballroom, probably did more to promote the Bradford Rock 'n' Roll scene than anyone at that time. His far sightedness and promotional skills were far in advance of his superiors.

him by sight. Only recently had he been made manager of the Gaumont Ballroom. Ray was an extremely nice guy who I believe would have gone far if left to his own devices, but events were to take place which would not allow this to happen. During our conversation he asked if our group would like a booking and was most surprised when I told him we were no more. Then, out of the blue, he asked if I would like the job as Disc Jockey working for him. With that, he proceeded to the stage where the group, the Mel Clarke Four, were just finishing their half-hour spot. He thanked them, then, sitting at the DJ stand, he casually played the records for the next half hour until Mel Clarke was re-introduced. Ray came off the stage towards me and explained, "You see Dal," (no one called me Derek) "I don't have the time to spend half the night up there playing Disc Jockey. I have a hundred and one things to do as manager." He said I would be required next Sunday, 7.30 pm until 10.30 pm, supervising the guest spots, arranging times of playing, introduction, and general chat through the microphone while introducing each record. Ray was the first to admit that he was

Your local DJ.

not the world's best Disc Jockey, but he had the ability to pull it off in his own way, which was short and to the point. For each of those nights I would be paid 30/- (£1.50) which, at today's value, would be around £20.00 per night. I remember I accepted almost immediately, thinking how easily Ray had completed the last half hour.

Ray had asked me to be there about 7.00 pm the next Sunday to go through the control system of the DJ stand and liaise with the guest group regarding performance times. Actually, Ray met me at the Wyke bus stop near Ruffield Side, as he just lived round the corner at Milner Ing. On reflection, it portrays those days quite well when, at a windswept bus stop in Wyke, the manager of the Gaumont Ballroom and Bradford's top DJ were standing waiting for a bus to take them to another world. When we arrived Ray took me to the DJ stand and for the first time I surveyed the equipment. Firstly, the DJ stand was just a large 2' x 2' cabinet about 4' high. On top was a normal deck, on/off switch and volume switch. You just placed the disc on, clicked the arm to the right to get the turntable going, then placed the arm by hand onto the disc, at the same time turning the volume up. At the left hand side was one of those Sixties-type wire record holders where the records were kept. A point that I was reminded of many times was that the cabinet was set on castors. There were two chairs, one for extra records and the other for me. As if all this was not enough to control, there was the microphone which was a huge heavy 1940s BBC type. Again, you switched this off by a switch on the microphone itself. Both the sound of the discs and microphone bellowed from massive amplifiers set up high to the ceiling each side of the stage. To this day I cannot remember who the guest group was on my first night. Ray helped me by going on from 7.30 pm until 8.00 pm. All this time I had been positioned in the chair next to him, noting his comments and his use of the turntable. Eight o'clock came and Ray, in his loud clear voice, introduced me. "And now . . . here's your new DJ for the future. Many of you know . . . Dal . . . Stevens". As this was going on I moved from the spare chair to the DJ chair. Ray had already taken the last played disc off and substituted another giving me a second to glance what it was, and mumbling something about 'good evening', I proceeded to put on the disc about half way through. My first disc was *Baby Sitting Boogie*. My palm was sweating holding the mike which was in my right hand, but my left hand had been almost uncontrollably trembling all over — hence the disc being put on half way through. Good old Ray, he had disappeared into the crowd so I was on my own. How simple he had made it look. The countdown was as follows:

1. Select disc, not any, but a popular one they could dance to.
2. Make sure you have the A-side the right way up.
3. Think of something to say pertaining to the record, also title and artist.
4. As the first disc ends, turn down the sound, comment "That was ... " etc.
5. Take first disc off, substituting new with ad-lib statements etc, and turn up the sound.

All this done with the left hand whilst the right hand held the mike, all in a few seconds. Then you had to choose, wait and repeat. This was Top Rank at its most technical 'Heath Robinson'. My second disc was almost started near the end and I commented without the mike being switched on. But I could only improve. By the time 8.30 pm came around I was just about in control. I found I could ad-lib pretty well, so before and after each record I had something to say, either about the disc, or forthcoming attractions. The crowds averaged five to six hundred on Sundays. I knew quite a few of the crowd because of my group-playing days and was looked on in some favour by most, but I still had the odd critics, troublemakers, and assortments. After a while I started a request time. People would come up and request a record. If we had it I would make a note of it and then announce it, similar to a radio request. Inevitably it did cause problems as some people would literally bounce up onto the stage and lean on the DJ cabinet (remember it was on castors). This would make the cabinet jump, in turn the turntable would jump two inches causing many irritated, inquisitive faces to glance up at the stage. This was done mostly by accident, but we did have the inevitable cretin who had to be reprimanded in no uncertain terms not to do it again or else. This had the desired effect and word soon spread that, although I liked a laugh, I did not suffer fools gladly. I remember one particular female who was a constant annoyance. She always stood with a crowd at the right hand of the stage. I have never had an inferiority complex, but she was getting to me. She was always there, gesticulating, making derogatory remarks, giggling, looking up and making comments. This was most disconcerting and I was beginning to dread seeing her each night. She was not particularly attractive and she was also quite plump. Then one evening I had had enough, this had to be stopped or it would go on indefinitely. So, when the guest group was on, which happened to be The Crusaders, I arranged that, during their performance, I would give out an appeal. This I did during a break in their numbers. I wandered to the front of the stage and announced "For a long time now there has been a young lady down here at the front of the stage who has just been longing every week to be able to sing with the guest group. So, let's have a big hand for J........ S.........". This was totally unexpected by her, she turned deep crimson, and quickly pushed her way back through the crowd to the rear of the ballroom. I said "Oh dear, she must have changed her mind. Well, maybe next time". She still came to the Gaumont, but I never saw her hanging around the stage again, especially when a guest group were playing, as she never knew when the "next time" was going to come.

Only one time at the Gaumont was I physically threatened, and he was drunk. During a break I was at the soft drinks bar when this stocky Scots guy came up and threatened me, because, he said, I had not played his girlfriend's request record. At this point the two doormen, Aubrey and Ken, in the form of the Cavalry arrived, picked up my aggressor, and literally threw him out. I thought no more about it until 10.30 pm. As we were closing Ray came in and told me that my friend was hanging about outside, promising he would get me on my way out. Ray said not to worry as he was getting a taxi and would see me home. The minute the taxi pulled up outside I was rushed down the steps surrounded by Ray, Aubrey and Ken. They literally threw me into the taxi. It resembled a scene from *The Untouchables*. As we sped away I noticed my Scots friend cowering in a doorway looking the other way. I had visions of another confrontation, but found out later he was in town on holiday.

Aubrey and Ken were both dependable stalwarts who could be relied upon in any situation, always looking very smart and alert in their evening suits, but in an emergency they were always there when required. Both were ex-KOYLI World War Two veterans and one of them, if not both, had received the Military Medal for Gallantry. After a few weeks I was beginning to feel I had been doing this for years. I was really enjoying myself. What next?

CHAPTER NINE

The Gaumont Scene

Built as part of the Cinema Project in the 1930s, the Gaumont Ballroom was set with a central entrance on New Victoria Street. Once up the steps and into the building, the ballroom was situated above the restaurant, overlooking Thornton Road. During the writing of this book, the old Gaumont Ballroom, which had been still hidden in the corner of the building has been refurbished into the Odeon Cinema Complex — another link gone.

Inside the Gaumont Ballroom.

The ballroom had one of the finest sprung floors in the country, but with the progress of Rock 'n' Roll, the nightly dances for ballroom dancers had lessened to Friday and Saturday, incorporating the occasional local business firm's annual dance. These were well presided over by the very popular Bert Bentley's Orchestra. Bert was another of nature's gentlemen, who always had a kind word to say, even though I was contributing to the change of scene from Bert's type of music.

With the popularity of Rock 'n' Roll at the Gaumont on Sunday (and the Majestic on Monday), another night was made available for it on Wednesday. This meant I now had two nights as the Disc Jockey, Sunday and Wednesday. While all these new innovations were taking place, my so called full-time career at Grattan came to an end. I felt a change must be made and, as two nights at the Gaumont would not make me rich, I had to find something that would give me time to fulfil my showbusiness fantasy.

For some six weeks I was out of work (a long time in those days, especially when the *Telegraph & Argus* situations vacant columns were overflowing). It was the only time in my life when I have had to sign on. I was nobody special, but I hated making my way up Nelson Street to the employment office to sign on. It was almost Christmas time, 1960, and a bad time to sign on because, in those days, if the snow came, everybody who was in this unfortunate position, was given a pick and shovel and transported around Bradford in lorries to clear snow — or no dole money.

During this time of financial embarrassment, my ever dependable Mum and Dad subsidised me, like all good parents do in times of crisis. I used to spend nearly every day down at the Gaumont Ballroom with the manager, Ray, who on many occasions would treat me for lunch in the restaurant. Thank you Ray! During all this time I was scanning the lunchtime edition of the *Telegraph & Argus's* situations vacant, hoping for a good position to suit my many talents. One day, there it was: "Wanted, van driver to deliver cycle accessories". The company was called Runwells (Do you?, people used to ask), which was a small cycle parts distributor for the West Riding (as it was then). I rang the number and received an appointment to call round; the building was on Union Street, at the back of the Castle Hotel. Within the hour I had been hired. The job was to collect all the parts ordered by the representative, place into boxes, and deliver the goods to all parts. The vehicle provided was an old type 7 cwt Thames van. The pay was £11 per week, 8.30 am to 5.00 pm. For anyone who has no ambition and was catering for low blood presure in later life, this was the ideal post. No stress, no target figures to achieve, just driving about delivering small cycle parts to the towns and villages in the Dales. There was only one rule which I had strictly to adhere to, and that was that I had to be back by five o'clock to lock the van away. Once that was done it was shanks's pony to catch the Wyke bus at the bottom of Manchester Road. I stayed two years with Runwells, and I was extremely happy and content.

I now had a full-time job and was a semi-pro Disc Jockey. On Sundays I could take my time getting down for the show at 7.30 pm. Usually I would be there about 7.00 pm to set the DJ stand up and to get all the records ready, test the PA system and most important of all, to check with the guest group the times on stage and the introductions required. On Wednesday the same procedure took place, the only difference being that to get there was a rush. Five o'clock, finish work, through town to the Wyke bus, 5.20 pm home. Tea, wash and change and be out again at 6.40 pm, and in town for about 7.00 pm. Luckily, the Gaumont being just across the road from the bus stop made things easier. This was to be my usual procedure, with more nights later, for the next four years, and most of the time by bus. Of course, the same situation arose on leaving the Gaumont on Sunday and Wednesday nights, to get the bus to

Wyke. As you can imagine 75% of the teenagers who were on that bus had been to the Gaumont. Earlier in the evening when I had been introducing the Pop Star of the day to them, I could control, advise or ridicule any one of the hundreds of teenagers in the ballroom, but on leaving the ballroom at 10.45 pm, walking for the bus, queueing at the stop and then on the bus, it was my turn to be controlled and ridiculed all the way home. Mostly though, it was good humoured, I think! "Dal, why didn't you play this?" "Dal, who is on next week?" "Dal, you are a rotten Disc Jockey", and so on. Still, if you can dish it out you should be able to take it back, as they say. It went with the job.

No-one had devised what Disc Jockeys should wear in those days; you could say it was optional. My only distinction was my waistcoat, but not any old waistcoat, this one was made of silver brocade enhanced with pearl buttons. This had materialised from the popular television programme *Maverick* starring James Garner or Jack Kelly. Both of them always wore this type of waistcoat, so to add to my wardrobe this was specially made up by a tailor residing in the Odeon precinct. This waistcoat, along with a frilly shirt from Hargreaves down Sunbridge Road, and my dark suit, was to be my trademark for the future. I thought at one time it might start a trend because of the many enquiries regarding my waistcoat, but it didn't.

Some of the hit numbers of that time which were popular were Frank Ifield's *I remember you,* Del Shannon's *Runaway,* Bobby Angelo's *Baby Sitting Boogie* and B Bumble and The Stingers *Nutrocker.* Whilst some of the records did make Number One if it was a ballad, they weren't really suitable to dance to; a slow number, however popular, soon cleared the dance floor. The choice of records was left to me, Ray Moore giving me a free hand. On Saturday mornings I would go up to Woods Music Shop in Sunbridge Road to select my choice.

MARTY WILDE

The staff were always very helpful and, of course, being teenagers themselves, their opinion of what was popular to dance to came in quite handy. One of the female staff who was particularly helpful was Barbara, who in the next few months, was to help change the DJ line-up.

The Wednesday night was proving to be very popular, but not as much as Sunday when we had the star celebrity. The stars who appeared were not at that time exactly top stars, but, in most cases, had some success in the charts. You still hear some of their names banded about from time to time, but others are long forgotten. But at the time in question they were popular enough to fill the Gaumont Ballroom on Sunday nights. Names like The Flintstones, Vince Eagar, Dickie Pride, The Spotnicks, Heinz, Rob Storme and The Whispers, The Barron Knights, Wee Willie Harris, Cliff Bennett and The Rebel Rousers, Sounds Incorporated, Screaming Lord Sutch, Zoot Money and His Big Roll Band, Ricky Valance *(Tell Laura I love her)*, Marty Wilde, Jess Conrad. Some remembered, some forgotten.

CHAPTER TEN

Tales of The Unexpected

Of the many stars of the time who appeared at the Gaumont, some I have forgotten, and best forgotten! Others have left their mark with me. Screaming Lord Sutch is well known now for his many standings for Parliament representing the Monster Raving Loony Party. He had made a couple of records comprising mainly of screams and shouts, and on this novelty, had made his mark with the teenagers and the 'angry young men brigade'. It was during my out-of-work period that he appeared at the Gaumont and, as I spent most of my time there; I was on hand to greet him on Sunday afternoon for his Sunday evening appearance.

WARNING (STOP) TAKE COVER (STOP) RAVING LUNATIC AT LARGE (STOP) YOU WILL NOT BE SAFE IN THIS HALL NEXT WEEK
Reward offered for recapture :- BAND BOX Productions, Southampton

Wide Boy Dave Sutch — and I was the mug!

Sutch was the wide boy and I was the mug. Greetings and formalities over, he asked where he could get a meal. The Alassio Restaurant above the Coffee Bar over the road, I informed him. "Would you care to join me", he said. "Yes", I replied. So over to the Alassio we went and ordered steak and chips, quite expensive at 7/6, followed by a sweet and tea (pot of). He was chatty and I was a good listener. I was fascinated by his reminiscences of the show business scene in London, which seemed like the other side of the world to me. Now remember he had asked me to join him, so when the bill was presented he picked it up, perused it, passed it to me, said "Thanks a lot", got up and walked out. 19/6 that meal cost me! Later, when we met up to arrange his evening performance, neither of us mentioned a thing about the meal.

Wee Willie Harris, I never understood a word he said!

With Wee Willie Harris I never understood a word he said, either during his performance, or in the dressing room. I can only say that whatever his poison, he could certainly move on that stage, complete with orange hair and leopard skin. He was a wonder and brought in the crowds.

My first of many meetings with the Barron Knights and Duke d'Mond was at the Gaumont. Duke d'Mond was the vocalist but this title was later dropped to just the Barron Knights.

One of the best performances I ever saw at the Gaumont was Cliff Bennett and The Rebel Rousers, along with Zoot Money and His Big Roll Band. These two groups were really a true echo of their discs; many performers sounded nothing like their recordings, showing that a lot of the so-called talent was abysmal without the assistance of the sophisticated equipment of the recording studio. Incidentally, Zoot Money went on to become a musical arranger with such accomplishments as *Tutti-Frutti* a 1980s television series.

The Spotnicks, a Swedish group, arrived on the scene, but the group, like the Sputnik, just drifted into space and were never heard of again.

The Spotnicks — Just drifted into space and were never heard of again . . .

Another product of the era was Heinz (not the soup!), in fact, Heinz Burt, ex bass player of The Tornados, of *Telstar* fame. A blonde guy with really vivid short-cropped hair. He produced a couple of so-called hits, but like so many in a similar vein, he did have a certain charisma that attracts the opposite sex. Needless to say, he created another full house at the Gaumont. We did not make an impression on each other, as I cannot remember any of our conversations. Heinz —where are you now? Still doing the circuits I see.

Ricky Valance *(Tell Laura I Love Her)* was a very unassuming and amiable person. I remember spending some two hours in his company after his Gaumont appearance. He was a little down and going through some problems with his latest girlfriend. It was hard to comprehend this guy being upset by a girl when at that time he could have had his pick of hundreds. He smoked all my cigarettes and told me I had made him feel better. I had consequently missed my last bus home, but again Ray Moore got me a taxi. About two weeks later I received a parcel at home, postmarked "London". Inside were two hundred cigarettes and a £5.00 note. On a card included was written "Many thanks Dal, All the best, Ricky". I had the impression that, like most pop stars of the 'One Night Stands', living out of a suitcase, he lacked company. I supposed he was back with his girlfriend, or some other.

His *Slippin' And Slidin'* hit number stunned the Gaumont teenagers.

Dickie Pride, now there is a name to conjure with, a product of the Jack Good stable. Sometimes when the television is showing old Rock 'n' Roll film clips, they include the one of Billy Fury, Marty Wilde and Dickie Pride singing *Three Cool Cats*. Sad to say, only Marty Wilde survives. Both Billy Fury and Dickie Pride passed away some time ago. I remember well Dickie Pride's performance at the Gaumont. Everybody stopped dancing to listen to him sing. He was really good, especially his hit number *Slippin' And Slidin'*. A few years later I noticed a photograph of Dickie in the newspaper with the headline "Ex-Rock'n'Roll Star Now Coalman. Yes, It's Dickie Pride Humping Coal Sacks Around".

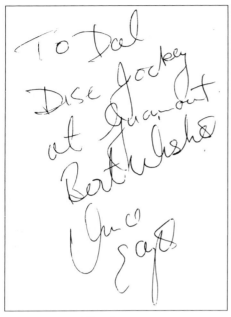

Vince Eager
— another who took a liking to my cigarettes!

Vince Eager was another guy who took a liking to my cigarettes. He was tall and stringy, like a bean pole (6'5"). His voice was most unusual. It had a kind of warbled effect, most effective with the ballad numbers. He had his moments on *Six-Five Special* but never really reached the top. The list was endless — names of yesteryear. Some survived for a few months on the success of a record, others managed a few years, then drifted onto the club circuit, a few passing away, but hopefully, not entirely forgotten.

While both the Majestic and Gaumont were under the Top Rank circuit, both had their own managers, Mr Lawrance at the Majestic and Ray Moore at the Gaumont, but this would change. Meanwhile, with the advent of another night at the Gaumont, I thought I might require some help. Then came my suggestion that perhaps my old pal, Terry Moran, would like to join me on both nights, like a double act. Terry, as previously explained, had left my group to join the Dingos, in which he had been quite successful. But, as with all the groups of that time, a change had been made and Terry was out. A name for Terry was required and Ray came up with 'Dadio' (pronounced Daddy-O). Terry did not complain and accepted it, so was born 'Dal and Dadio'. Terry and I got on famously, although a problem did occur in that Terry had recently had a burst ulcer which caused a secondary effect of alopecia. With this he lost all his hair, giving an effect more like father and son rather than Dal and Dadio. With great courage he faced those many teenagers with me for the next two months until his hair had grown back. Like myself, within a few weeks he had adapted himself to the new situation, which was no problem as he was used to performing to a large audience. His style, though, was in sharp contrast to

'Dal and Dadio': 1961
- more like father and son!

mine. While I tried to give myself what was called a 'Trans-Atlantic accent', Terry used a deep mellow voice not unlike that of Brian Matthew. In fact, many were the comments made that he sounded like Brian Matthew (well known in the Sixties on *Saturday Club*, etc).

With Terry and I together again, we were soon running a very professional show. Needless to say, when the groups had been introduced for their half hour performance, we would nip across the road to Viv's Bar for a quick pint. Looking back it seems funny to be running a show for, perhaps, one thousand teenagers, but actually be stood chatting in a bar while it ran itself. But, during all those years, I cannot remember coming back to a problem. The problems always seemed to occur when we were there. One particular night the microphones would not work, although the turntables would. We were most embarrassed, just sitting putting the records on with nothing to say. The guest group which were The Crusaders could only play their instruments.

With the innovation of Wednesday, lots of local groups were required. Some were good and some were not, but all were enthusiastic and good friends, as it was generally on our recommendation to Ray as to whether they were offered another booking. While some were only mediocre, all were given another chance. In offering another booking we also had to take into account the audience's reaction, especially the females. More about them in a later chapter.

CHAPTER ELEVEN
Politics — All Change!

I had hoped that this scene was set to continue for many months, if not years, but alas, all good things must come to an end. Ray came up with another idea. Why not have some nice attractive girl on stage who could sit with us and make out requests as well as have the record handy to play. One girl who immediately sprung to mind was Barbara, who worked at Woods' Records and in that capacity could work well with both of us for, as well as being attractive, she was most conversant with the pop scene.

Barbara joined us just for the Wednesday nights. Ray gave her the name Della, so now it was 'Dal, Della and Dadio'. So, with Della sat in the middle of us, she was soon accepted by the teenagers and contributed well to the act. But things were to change, and very quickly too. Ray was on his way out. A new General Manager was appointed for both the Majestic and the Gaumont. He came up from 'South of Watford' to make the inevitable changes. Bob Mitchell was his name and I could tell by his attitude towards Ray that Ray would not be with us for long. After a very short time Ray left. Mr Mitchell's comments were to the effect that he did not want Ray Moore's name mentioned in his presence again, and what is more, it wasn't long before Mr Lawrance left the Majestic.

Thus we lost two very well-thought-about gentlemen. Mitchell was not a fan of teenagers or their music. His god was Bingo, and what happened in those few weeks would set the trend for the next few years for the decline of the dance halls in favour of Bingo. My instructions first of all, were that the booking of stars for Sunday night would stop. Also, the buying of records had to stop.

Bob Mitchell. He arrived from South of Watford to make inevitable changes.

All this time we had been able to select the records we required from Woods. We had always been quite frugal and only bought the records which were necessary, which were popular, and were what the teenagers would dance to. These always included the top of the charts because these were what the teenagers requested.

This was to be no more. When records were requested we had to make some feeble excuse and change the subject. Mitchell was choking the dance hall business to death, running it down, phasing it out. I argued with Mitchell that he was putting us in a ridiculous situation with no current record to hand. He reluctantly gave us permission to buy three new records a week. Of course, this was not enough and our record collection became a source of never-ending embarrassment. These facts need relating because of what they did to the Bradford Rock 'n' Roll scene and, with the situation as it was, others would take advantage. As Mitchell was also in charge of the Majestic, the situation there was likewise. The Majestic had no regular DJ at this time, Garth Cawood of Dingos fame was filling in.

It was during a visit one Monday night to the Majestic when I was passing Mitchell surveying all his domain on the balcony, that he asked me out of the blue if I would like to be DJ at the Majestic also, just me, no Dadio. I told him I would as I knew Terry would not mind — we had already discussed our course of action should the situation arise. I never trusted Mitchell, he only told you what he wanted you to know. I knew from snippets of conversation and the odd slip of the tongue that he was dismantling the ballroom scene, even though it was enjoying a fair degree of success. And for what? On the blue, two little ducks, twenty-two!

For the time being things carried on at the Gaumont: Sundays and Wednesdays, but minus Della, another casualty who left because Mitchell said she was surplus to requirements. He had no such thoughts regarding Terry. As a team he seemed to like us. So, with Della gone, we were left to run the show ourselves. He admitted that he was not interested in the music scene, so that's what we did, ran it ourselves.

We were still being paid 30/- each per night, not bad money for Mr Mitchell, paying £6.00 for someone else to run the show and keep over one thousand teenagers happy for two nights a week. Luckily, we kept on the local groups and managed a return visit for the Barron Knights, but only because they had been pre-booked before the change over.

Ray moving on left a great void, especially his contributions during the last few months of bringing new stars to the scene, and introducing competitions for the teenagers.

One of his last stars to appear on Sunday was Rob Storme. This was during a special Drinka Pinta Milk Week. After the show Rob posed with some of the local girls holding their glasses of milk. A few days later at the Odeon Cinema I received a tap on the shoulder during the interval. It was Rob Storme with a local girl. He said he was appearing in Newcastle the following day and this young lady happened to be his current girlfriend. I saw her many times later at the Majestic, but no Rob. He, like many others, just faded from the pop scene.

Winner of our Miss Personality Contest, Joyce Harvey, receives a £5 prize from Tony, Assistant Manager, while the runners-up look on.

Competitions had become a feature during Ray Moore's time. These usually took place as jive contests. Most times it was either me or Dadio that did the judging and it never seemed to escape the notice of the teenagers that the winning competitors were usually the prettiest (not the fellas!) and that Dal or Dadio were often seen later escorting the winners to the pictures or coffee bars! Prizes ranged from compacts for the ladies, brush and comb sets for the gents, and sometimes free tickets for the coming shows. Nothing really fantastic, although on one occasion five pounds (over half a week's salary) for the winner of the 'Miss Personality Contest'. We were just trying

Rob Storme with some of the Gaumont's regulars. The occasion was 'Drinka Pinta Milk Week'. (Courtesy Telegraph & Argus).

Rob Storme presents prize to Hazel and Dennis Richardson, winners of the Jive Competition for Drinka Pinta Milk Week. Manager Ray Moore looks on.

Diana Winnard. Winner of the Gaumont's Miss Bellair Competition.

to introduce something a bit different. One such evening which springs to mind was a hair style competition to be judged during the course of the evening by none other than "Raymond" otherwise known as "Mr Teasy-Weasy". A real scoop for Ray Moore. I still don't know how he managed to arrange it. Raymond had no hesitation in selecting the winner — Miss Diana Winnard from Bankfoot, who collected the prize of a year's supply of Bellair hair spray or lacquer, an absolute must for the hairstyles of the day. Bellair being the company promoting the product. The lucky winner's photograph (see above) appeared in the *Telegraph & Argus* the next day.

'Miss Lovely Legs' was another of my ideas, but the problem was getting the girls to take part. You had to be very careful, especially if the girl had a boyfriend, as, in order to enter, I would have to ask the girl if she would like to take part. That is, of course, after I had checked her suitability for the competition. Nothing has changed from that day to this in that a guy can become quite ruffled if his girlfriend is ogled.

It was harmless fun, but it could have its problems. We had to be extra careful in those days, more so with the legs competition as it was the days of suspenders and our Miss Lovely Legs could only show the leg from just above the kneecap. Finally, we managed to persuade ten local girls to enter. Judging this competition did have its drawbacks. You could win a friend and make nine enemies, so on this occasion we managed to acquire the services of Dennis Mitchell, the well known Bradford wrestler who was a very popular TV celebrity at the time. The girls were lined up on the stage, skirts were lifted above the kneecap (to the obvious delight of the guys in front of the stage), Dennis made his choice, the girl blushed, Dennis handed her the prize (two free tickets for the next Gaumont Theatre Package show), and kissed her on the cheek. This was all done for the convenience of the photographer from the *Telegraph & Argus* and the next night the photograph would be in the paper.

(During my research for this book I made enquiries regarding the many photographs taken by the paper of similar competitions at the Gaumont and the Majestic during this time. It appears no copies were kept. A sad loss for future generations).

Solo Bop. What does that conjure up? This was purely for the male. It comprised of the guy jiving or bopping on his own, legs girating, bouncing about, and an occasional splits thrown in. Most ballrooms or dance halls banned this derivative of Rock 'n' Roll simply because of the problems it could cause if physical contact was made with the routinely dancing couples. The same law ruled at the Gaumont and Majestic, but from time to time we gave the solo bop enthusiasts a five minute spot to dance on their own with no danger of colliding with anyone else. The lads really enjoyed this, just as we did watching them, usually to some fast instrumental number. Everyone's favourite whilst solo bopping was 'Radar'. Even today some people still ask "Do you remember Radar?" Every dance hall of the time had its character and we had Radar. He was known and loved by everybody, and I do mean everybody. He stood about 5'6" tall and was always dressed in a dark suit with 14" bottoms, the usual thick crepe soled shoes, and a narrow dark tie on white shirt. He had a round boyish face adorned with short dark brown curly hair. I would not say he was a ladies' man or even that he was particularly good looking, he was just a nice unassuming lad of the times blessed with a very fortunate disposition. He was generally the instigator of the request for the Solo Bop spot and when he was in action everybody would crowd around to watch him move. Needless to say, Radar won a prize every week, if not a competition or spot prize then we would invent a reason for giving him a prize. Some said it was strange how Radar seemed to have a birthday every other week. Just the mention of his name over the mike was met with resounding cheering and clapping. I occasionally see him around the town, he works for Bradford Council and I know that many of his fans will be pleased to

Radar. Over the years many names are forgotten, but of all the patrons who attended the Majestic and Gaumont Ballrooms, Radar is remembered by everyone.

know that he is looking very well and has hardly changed.

With reference to his nickname, nobody knows where this materialised, even Radar is unsure how he obtained it!

From the loveable face of Radar to another well known, or should I say notorious Bradford character, who thankfully only occasionally showed his face at the dances, Jacky Binns. Jacky's reputation went before him. Jacky had had a few skirmishes with the police and, as this was common knowledge, people would tread warily when he was around, give him a wide berth. On Jacky's visits, more so at the Gaumont, I could sense when he arrived. A hesitant quietness would preside over the music, then, towards the back of the hall would emerge the tall wiry figure of Jacky, probably with another couple of well-knowns sidling through the crowd. During the few times he did pay us a visit he never caused any trouble at all, although you could see the apprehension on the faces of the doormen. On one occasion he appeared while the group were playing and as Dadio and myself were acquainted with him we joined him and his beautiful girl at his table. During the course of our conversation the young lady kept interrupting Jacky and pestering him for a soft drink. Jacky's retort was thunderous, " .... off when I'm talking to my mate", in other words, "Keep quiet!" We laughed about it later as it just reminded us of some Al Capone type with his moll in down town Chicago. But this was Jacky's style. On another occasion a fight had started outside the Alassio, across the road from the Gaumont. It appeared that two young thugs were giving a policeman a hard time, indeed, the policeman had received a blow that had rendered him unconscious. Jacky had witnessed what had happened and collared the two culprits who then set about him! In the meantime, police reinforcements from the Town Hall arrived and, disregarding the two lads fighting Jacky, waded into him and hauled him away laughing. Luckily, before Jacky was charged, the injured policeman had regained consciousness in time to point the finger at the real villains.

I know Jacky will not mind me relating these tales because, as with Radar, he still stands out in people's memories of that era.

CHAPTER TWELVE

Farewell The Gaumont

At this time the Barron Knights were very popular in Bradford and looked on with favour when playing at the Gaumont. This was, of course, before the advent of their hit record *Call Up The Groups* in the mid-Sixties which brought them national fame. Always good for a laugh, they would ask Dadio and myself to join them for a number, sometimes as a duet or myself just singing *Whole Lotta Shakin' Goin' On* and Dadio accompanying me on the piano for this number with the Barron Knights backing. At the end of the shows we would discuss future plans, in fact, we developed quite a good relationship with them, good pals in fact, which lasted until they made the big time.

From Hull came Lee Walker and The Travellers who became firm favourites with the crowd. With them also appeared a singer called Brian Rossi, a flamboyant, leather-clad medallion-swinging type who sang out of key — the females loved him.

Brian Rossi. Brian appeared with Lee Walker and The Travellers. He sang out of key, the females loved him.

The Karl Denver Trio produced a change for one show, making a most pleasant evening singing the number four Top Twenty hit *Wimoweh*. I will always remember Karl Denver for his courtesy on and off the stage. The singing group The Viscounts of *Thank Your Lucky Stars* fame came,

LEE WALKER AND THE TRAVELLERS

Firm favourites from Hull at both the Gaumont and later the Majestic.

and went into oblivion. Through all this Dal and Dadio performed on the Sunday and Wednesday, augmented on one occasion, by a big fight that developed. This, as stated, was not usual. It is vivid in my memory because a knife was thrown at the DJ stand during the melee and actually stuck into the backdrop about two feet above Dadio's head. Surely we were not that bad! Another particular instance I remember was noticing at the back of the dance hall, by the soft drinks bar, a rather tall well-dressed gentleman. He was speaking to the manager of the cinema which was incorporated in the same building. I knew the manager well as he used to let me in the Gaumont Cinema free during my relaxation times with a girlfriend. As I was passing the bar during my break the cinema manager called me over and introduced me to Mr Peter Arne. Mr Arne asked if I was American as he'd noticed during my performances that I spoke with an American accent (my trans-Atlantic accent). It did not take but a couple of sentences into our conversation for him to perceive that I was pure West Riding. I did not give the conversation a second thought until years later the Peter Arne I was introduced to was a film star appearing in many films. He was a homosexual and was murdered by one of his lovers in 1983.

But the end was coming. Towards the end of 1961 a new idea came forth for Saturdays. For some years Bert Bentley and his Orchestra had been resident at the Ballroom. Now was proposed four and three quarter hours of non-stop entertainment, with Dal and Dadio doing a couple of spots, also an hour of jazz and Benny Netherwood's Wool City Jazzmen. All this for 5/-. As it was, things worked out quite well and like all new ideas, the first attendances looked like it could be a winner. But Christmas came and went, the crowds again started to slip away, and disappointing Saturdays helped to sway the decision towards Bingo. Sunday and Wednesday 'Big Beat' nights were still going strong. We still had capacity crowds and, while not offering top line groups, our own established groups were holding their own. We had our usual Christmas Show with no money to spend, but the place had been decorated very well and we were supplied with two hundred balloons to blow up and assemble in the nets high above the dance floor, ready to drop at a moment's notice. We were also furnished with two huge boxes containing spot prizes — wallets, brush sets, compacts, etc.

The courteous Karl Denver Trio. Note the autograph: To Dal, Our Best Disk Jockey!

Saturday Spectacular

IT'S NEW ! IT'S GREAT ! ! IT'S SENSATIONAL ! ! !

and it's at the Top Rank Ballroom

Gaumont - Bradford

FIRST with up to date Entertainment

Saturday, 25th November 1961

7.0 to 11.45   *Admission 5/-*

Three Great Attractions 4¾ hours entertainment

7.0 p.m. *to* *8.0 p.m.*	Dal and Dadio, the craziest Disc Jockeys The Best R'n'R in Bradford
8.0 p.m. *to* *9.0 p,m.*	Bert Bentley & His Orchestra featuring Bradford's Latest Resident Vocalist George Fisher
9.0 p.m. *to* *10.0 p.m.*	It's Trad Jazz at its best provided by Benny Netherwood & the Wool City Jazzmen Featuring Kathie Mickleson—Blues Singer
10.0 p.m. *to* *11.45 p.m.*	We provide Bert Bentley & His Orchestra Dal, Dadio and George Fisher with 1¾ hours of good class entertainment **FOR YOU**

The Saturday Spectacular ran until after Christmas. *The last show coincided with the closure of the ballroom.*

The end came a few weeks after Christmas. The announcement was short and to the point. The ballroom was closing, probably to promote Bingo (which it did for a short while). While our many loyal friends were disappointed, they knew they could continue up at the Maj (Majestic) where many were already going on Mondays, so they were not too put out. In fact, the closing of the Gaumont Ballroom did not cause much consternation at all. The *Telegraph & Argus* didn't even give it a mention. Only many years later when it was found to be in a dilapidated state, was it spoken of with nostalgia.

We had our last Sunday and then Wednesday, and the very last show was to be the Saturday Spectacular. The Saturday arrived, a little better attended as some had come for that last dance on the famous sprung floor. Bert Bentley finished at 11.30 pm and I had the last fifteen minutes to play out to the few who stayed on, so, in a way, I was the last person to perform at the Gaumont Ballroom. The last number to ring out was Don Gibson's *Sea of Heartbreak*.

CHAPTER THIRTEEN
Goin' T' Maj?

During this time I had made my debut at the Majestic Ballroom. It was still for only one night, as the rest of the week was devoted to modern dancing which was still popular for the older ones (as teenagers would say, over-21s). Billy Hey's Orchestra contributed to some of the other nights. On Mitchell's request to take over, I had done the following Monday. Here the problems would be fewer, although I would be playing to more people, most of whom I knew, as they had been regular attenders of the Gaumont. The main entrance was situated half-way up Morley Street. It was still the same until the recent Alhambra renovations. Through the main entrance and to the right brought you straight into the ballroom. On each side of the stage and at the rear of the ballroom were tables and chairs. Up the steps by the entrance you would find a long balcony which encircled the dance floor and housed the soft drinks bar. Along the left hand side there were more tables and chairs. In between there was a staircase which led down to the left hand side of the dance hall. The capacity was 1,200 and some nights it would be filled. At the back of the large stage stood a two foot plinth which was the Disc Jockey stand. This was a complete double-deck unit. Although modern, the principle was the same as the Gaumont. This also applied to the hand mike, so the method of introduction need not alter. One change that was really beneficial was the lighting, this being controlled by Bill, whose windowed box overlooked the drinks bar in the balcony. This was an excellent observation point to control all the lighting of the ballroom, coloured lights, starlight scenes, everything to suit whatever was happening down below, and not forgetting the searching spotlight to highlight those special moments.

ABOVE: The front of the Majestic Ballroom in its Bingo days (1965-1969). Now a rehearsal room for the Alhambra.
(Photo: Tony Moss and Kevin Wheelan, courtesy of G J Mellor *The Cinemas of Bradford*).

RIGHT: Billy Hey, whose orchestra kept the over 21s happy with the alternative modern dancing at the Majestic.

Admission was 2/- (10p), 7.30 pm to 10.30 pm, for which you were entertained by the DJ for two hours, and the guest group for two half hour spots. While I would have overall responsibility, control of the crowd was from another quarter, namely the doormen (not bouncers), all well remembered by the many patrons. Sandy the Scot who was always looking at his watch at 10.30 pm and shouting "Come on Dal, get a move on, wind up, I wanna gi' home". Tall elegant Jim who was the spitting image of Sean Connery. Good looking Laurie and the rest who made up this competent band of dinner-suited peace-keeping officers.

From my vantage point on the stage I could spot any trouble immediately, so, at the slightest hint of unrest, I would turn down the sound of the record and announce "doormen on the floor". The words would have hardly left my lips when they had converged on the trouble from all sides, confidently sorting any problem before it got out of hand.

This, then, was the Majestic scene, where, not many months before, I had appeared with my group. Now I was back, but this time running the show. I had taken over as stated whilst still with Dadio down at the Gaumont. The change over was no problem and, after a couple of weeks, I felt I had been there for years. Being with more or less the same crowd helped. Also, Mitchell's attitude seemed to mellow somewhat. With him running down the Gaumont, he was spending most of his time at the Majestic and, out of the blue, through a London agency, he booked some recording stars. When I say stars, they didn't shine very brightly. These were pop singers who had produced some small hit, nothing more. They then went on circuits like ours to promote themselves.

Danny Rivers and The Rivermen made a Top Twenty hit, but were soon forgotten.

The first pop star of this calibre to arrive was Danny Rivers, recording for Decca. Of course, not many of our teenagers knew him so, while he went down quite well, he was soon to be forgotten. Likewise with Ricky Barron. Barry James was different in that he had a type of showband. He made quite a few return dates. Another group that springs to mind was Nero and The Gladiators, clad in Roman type togas. I remember all those mentioned with affection. They were really great guys. They were no different to any regular guy in the street except by the fact that they had made a record. One or two did appear later in the occasional TV show. It seemed strange to watch them on television and think "I compered his show when he came to Bradford."

Ricky Barron - a smoothy for the girls.

Barry James appeared a few times at the Majestic with his show band. They always gave a professional show.

Inside the Majestic (1962). One of the few photographs to survive which shows the inside during a show. The group are The Dakotas with Dave Arran.

In my capacity as DJ, a certain amount of respect was shown to me by these stars, and the feeling was reciprocated. Although they were the stars of the show, they knew that it would pay dividends to negotiate amicably with me for their introductions, times on, times off, etc. A good introduction from me would help enhance their act. You did come across the odd big-head who would strut around the stage displaying the "I'm better than you" attitude, but he would sooner or later get his wings clipped. But, on the whole, most were nice, pleasant, efficient people. Even if never seen again, I could say we were friends and colleagues in show business.

The company 7 cwt van I used, although never for my own use, I supposedly had to keep clean. This I was often instructed to do as it was always full of graffiti. Not the modern type, but mostly finger marks in the dust, stating "Dal Majestic Disc Jockey". "We love you Dal", and other such drivel, all inscribed by yours truly. What would a modern-day psychiatrist think of this?

So, after the few weeks on my own at the Majestic, the Gaumont had closed. It was no longer Dal and Dadio, my partner was not required at the Majestic, even with the closure of the Gaumont. So, I was still on my own at the Majestic. How long would this last? I was developing such a pessimistic attitude. If only I had known that the next three years would surpass all the rest.

CHAPTER FOURTEEN
The First of Many

A few weeks later I was asked my opinion of opening Wednesdays and Fridays, same type of show, more top line stars. Yes, as well as Monday! Was he asking or telling? This was the same person who helped to end an era at the Gaumont Ballroom. Now he was asking me to do about three nights at the Majestic. "Yes," I said "that would be great, but I would probably need Dadio back with me". "Leave it a few weeks," he said "and I'll get the ball rolling." So I did just that and concentrated on the Mondays. Why? Because he had just booked Joe Brown for the Monday.

It was to be Joe Brown's first appearance in Bradford and, as well as frequently being seen on television, he was currently having a string of hits which were equally good for dancing to. A particular one being *A Picture of You.* The pre-publicity for his appearance was all of a sudden very professional. We had good write ups in the *Telegraph & Argus* and the *Melody Maker*, both by Stan Pearson of the *Telegraph.* It was Stan who contributed some quite good publicity for us during this time, as long as we played his request, the Shadows' *Apache.*

A Monday night was fixed for this star. On that day I dropped in during the afternoon. As with most professional groups, they often arrived at this time to organise themselves. When this was done they could rest before their appearance, eat, and probably have a drink. So, everything was in order when the first customers came through into the ballroom. Occasionally the guest group would arrive late and had to sort out drums and equipment during my first hour. Most unprofessional, I never liked that.

Joe's group had already arrived. He would follow later. Being the star all he had to do was turn up. I introduced myself to his group, The Bruvvers, and clarified the time he would appear, 8.30 to 9.30 pm. Joe arrived later, a most amiable guy and very chatty. It seemed he had got lost driving here and ended up in Wakefield. No problems regarding time, he would be on stage when I requested. Asking if there were any nearby places to eat, I suggested Seabrook's Fisheries just out of the back door. Bruvver Peter Oakham asked if I would like to join them. I recalled a similar situation with Lord Sutch and gracefully declined, apart from which, I had to go home and change and return for the evening show at 7.00 pm.

Upon my return I found everything in order, The Bruvvers had returned from Seabrook's looking full and content, while Joe was sound asleep on the large settee in the dressing room. Access to these two dressing rooms was through a double door at the left hand side of the stage, so a mat-

Joe Brown

Majestic 1962

Joe gave me a lift home.

ter of a few yards had to be negotiated on the dance floor to the side of the stage when the entertainers made their entrance. It was then they would be most vulnerable to be touched or torn apart, whatever. Most times, the doorman linked arms and made a passage to run through. One change had been made in my absence. Mr Mitchell would introduce Joe Brown and The Bruvvers on stage. Just before the doors were open, six large settees were placed strategically all around the stage in the hope that they would serve as a barrier against the marauding hands trying to grab our guests. We had used this exercise once before with one of the minor groups and it had proved successful, and so the procedure was adopted as the norm when the more famous names appeared at the Majestic. There was no pre-sale of tickets then, so it was no surprise to me when earlier I had walked up Morley Street and saw the queue of excited teenagers six deep stretching down to the Alhambra, round the corner, and well out of sight; that there would be a capacity crowd of well over one thousand. Of course, the admission charge for this night had been increased to 5/- (25p). Mr Mitchell said it was the most the management had paid to date for a Pop Star (£200.00). He was now doing what poor old Ray Moore had been endeavouring to do for months. He was talking as if he had just discovered the adage 'Speculate to accumulate'.

I started at 7.30 pm in the usual style. At 8 o'clock I generally wished everyone a good evening and that I would now take requests. The crowd was indeed a capacity — a thousand teenagers girating around the floor. From my vantage point I looked out on a sea of bobbing heads, yet the hair motionless as the gallons of lacquer previously applied did its job on the back-combed tresses of the girls adorning their pretty pan-stick coated cheeks, and heavily mascara'd eye lashes: a swell of perspiring bodies working themselves up to a frenzy. Towards 8.30 pm the crowd began to drift closer to the stage to position themselves behind the barrier of settees. So, at the front of the stage people were already ten deep. A ruse I used many times in this situation was to announce at the end of a record "And now, the moment you have all been waiting for". On hearing this, the crowd, fully expecting the star to be announced, surged forward, the girls screaming in anticipation, and all that would happen was that I would introduce another record, causing many derogatory and justified remarks, mostly good humoured, to be directed at me. With a few minutes to go Joe's group, The Bruvvers, emerged from the dressing room, through the crowd and onto the stage, minus Joe of course, as they had to plug in ready for his appearance. This done, I played the last disc and handed over to Mitchell to introduce the star, which would usually only take a few seconds. But Mitchell had to make a meal of it and drift into a speech. "This was the first time this act had been to Bradford and there would be many more such great acts to follow —I would be grateful if you did not climb onto the stage." — on and on.

All this time Peter and The Bruvvers were poised for their intro for Joe and, as can be imagined, no-one was paying attention to what Mitchell was saying, and really no-one could hear or care as the noise was tremendous. From my position on the DJ stand I motioned to Pete to start the intro, which he did, drowning out Mitchell who was still rambling on. As the music rang out

Mitchell had to vacate the stage in haste, almost colliding with Joe on his way up. Joe grabbed the mike and went straight into one of his earlier hits *The Darktown Strutters Ball*. Of course, this brought the house down. For the next hour Joe progressed magically through his repertoire, which included numbers from musicals like *Oklahoma* and *Bye Bye Birdie*, as well as a subtle hint of religion with his brilliant rendition of *All Things Bright and Beautiful*. Another highlight was a rivetting *Hava Nagila*, climaxing with Joe plucking his guitar held behind his head. His final number was *Picture of You* which brought the show to a close.

Follow that! A few minutes before I had made my way back to my stand ready to say thank you and take over, as you cannot have a vast silence for a few minutes after the guest star has finished. So, with a thank you to Joe and The Bruvvers I led into the next record. Joe dived off the stage, through a gap in the crowd made by the sturdy doormen. I had an hour to play out, throughout which I was bombarded with autograph books to take to Joe and have signed. At 10.30 pm I finished the session, but for once there was quite a few hundred still in, mainly girls queueing for their coats, but there were quite a number around the stage dressing room door waiting for Joe. I took the many autograph books to him which he duly signed (it's surprising how some cannot be bothered). I distributed these to the fans and returned to the dressing room. By this time it was almost 11 o'clock and I had missed the last bus home. Joe asked me for directions out of Bradford to get onto the A1. I said where I lived in Wyke was en route to the A1, but I would be able to show him better on the way. Saying goodbye to The Bruvvers, who were still packing up, we made our way to where Joe had parked his car, most of the fans had left by now. The car was a mid-Fifties red sports model, not particularly flashy but, as Joe said, she was a goer. Off we sped through Bradford and up Manchester Road. A few minutes later we had reached my destination. Joe politely refused a cup of tea because of the long journey that lay ahead, made possibly longer by, yes, you've guessed, Huddersfield Road was not quite the direction to take for the A1 in those days. I vaguely pointed towards Brighouse and watched him drive away. Well, I thought, he has £200.00 in his back pocket and I've made 30/-, surely I qualify for a free ride home — needs must. Sorry Joe —a great guy!

CHAPTER FIFTEEN

Melodies, Requests and New Friends

Much of the nightly show comprised the playing of records, and like the artistes, many were forgotten; but similarly, some retain nostalgic memories. A record that instantly springs to mind is *Who's Chicken?* This was not actually the title, the title being *Newcastle Twist,* a rapid guitar/ Saxophone instrumental by Lord Rockingham's XI. It was frequently requested from the Solo Bop brigade, along with the really experienced jiving couples who could keep pace. During the playing of this record I would turn up the speed with intermittent shouts through the mike of "Who's Chicken?" directed at the dancers who fell by the wayside (couldn't keep up as the pace raced on).* Finally, the record would finish at an almost uncontrollable speed with hardly anyone left on the dance floor. Another was *Walk Right In, Sit Right Down.* Another, *Just Walk On By, Wait On The Corner.* We substituted the words with "Wait by the Town Hall". At this point we would turn down the sound and all the crowd retorted "Wait by the Town Hall", always good for a giggle. Jimmy Jones's *Good Timing,* Johnny Kidd's *Shaking All Over,* Johnny Tillotson's *Poetry in Motion*, Floyd Cramer's *On the Rebound, Runaway* — Del Shannon, *Nutrocker* by B Bumble and The Stingers. All these and many more were great favourites of the Majestic crowd, supplemented by the very great hits of Elvis Presley, Cliff Richard and The Shadows, during this period.

I had never really bothered with a signature tune, since, starting at 7.30 pm, people were just arriving. It was only around 8 o'clock I would say "Good Evening" and ask for requests. As usual, with most environments of this type, people had come to dance, and with jiving, a particular beat was required. I've known the floor to be packed with jivers which would immediately disperse to the sound of a slow Number One ballad that had been requested, as no-one could dance to it. No beat — just a ballad. Therefore, I tried to keep clear of such numbers, but on occasions I had to play the odd one which I generally terminated halfway through. There were certain numbers I did like to finish or play out with, Ray Anthony's *Walking Alone at Night* or The Cascades *Listen to The Rhythm of The Falling Rain.* Most people identified this with the end of the evening. People strolled off to the cloakroom, leaving the odd smooching couples still gliding along. Over and above the music I would be giving out notices of forthcoming attractions and at the very end finishing with "Goodnight Everyone, Goodnight!"

* Who's Chicken: meaning who's a coward or scared. This was a 1950s statement interjected into our vocabulary by the new generation of teenagers, quoted time and again in the many delinquent type American films of that era. If the so-called dare or challenge was not taken up then cries of "Chicken" would erupt and possibly the victim being subjected to clucking hen-like noises to motivate the hesitant unfortunate into doing some irresponsible act, sometimes with fatal results. This, I might add, never occured at the Majestic.

Jerry Lee Lewis. He was being hounded by the Press at the time.

This was usually concluded with the doormen closing and locking the doors or sometimes, if I had been running late, Bill in his soundproof box would turn most of the lights out and switch the mike off, as he had overall control.

Stars of another kind visited Bradford, but not the Majestic. The huge Gaumont had some of the large package shows - Buddy Holly, Cliff Richard, and there would be more, but this particular one was at St George's Hall. Jerry Lee Lewis and Johnny Kidd and The Pirates on the same bill. Being the DJ for Top Rank influenced my ability to actually meet them. I watched the show from the balcony, which also contained about every local group I knew. I was with my ex-group member Michael Farrell and Spike of the Dingos. During the interval of a fantastic show, we made our way to the stage rear, complete with security people. "Nobody can come through here" was the shout. As luck would have it I was recognised by one of the organisers who shuffled the three of us through. Jerry Lee Lewis had just returned to his dressing room. At the same time the security guards were busy frogmarching out a certain manager-come-singer of a local popular group! No names please! At the door was Jerry Lee, who asked us in. There was nobody else in the room so for the next fifteen minutes we had his complete attention.

His conversation was enlightening and exhilarating. He had been a hero of mine from my army days. Spike was also excited as his style of playing was similar to Jerry Lee's. Whiskies were offered and both Mike and Spike nearly finished the bottle. To say Jerry Lee had been going through a bad time was an understatement. The papers had a lot to say as, in America, he had recently married his thirteen year old cousin Myra and, while this was legal in the Southern states, it was rather frowned upon over here.

With other people now converging, we asked if we could visit Johnny Kidd. Jerry happily complied with our request and took us through an adjoining door to him. Here again was another of my favourites who chatted quite freely as he dried himself down. Johnny Kidd in costume was a remarkable act to see. Dressed in leather-type pirate costume — large thigh-high boots, his shirt with frills and lace. Also as a gimmick he wore a black eye patch. I still have the one he wore that night. It was during the chat in his dressing room that Michael felt the need to use the toilet. Johnny said the toilet was outside along the corridor, but no-one could get in or out because of the crowds of people milling about. So Johnny suggested that Mike use the wash basin, which he did with relief. Vulgar, but true. I never did meet Jerry Lee Lewis again despite making return visits to this country. Likewise with Johnny Kidd. Like his idol, Gene Vincent, Kidd would Rock 'n' Roll 'em over with a sweaty intensity rarely experienced in British pop before 1962. He was also one of the home-grown rockers who didn't go smooth at a time when the UK charts were riddled with 'Brilliantined Bobbies' and 'Regular Rickies' from across the Atlantic.

Liberties taken at Johnny Kidd's "Convenience"!!

Though his impact took place at the beginning of the Sixties, Johnny Kidd and his Pirates managed to stay afloat until his untimely death in a road accident near Preston in Lancashire in October 1966.

CHAPTER SIXTEEN
The Reunited Duo

With the success of the Joe Brown evening, Mitchell not only began to book other top liners, but, as he had mentioned a few weeks earlier, with the Gaumont now closed, the Majestic would now also open on Wednesdays and Fridays, which was indeed good news. This would involve me running three shows, mostly with our local groups, but with the occasional star like Joe Brown. Whilst this was acceptable, I did think I should have some help, and suggested that Dadio should help me again. Mitchell agreed. So, within a few weeks of the Gaumont closing, Dadio was to be back in the chair alongside me. We each received 30/-, which never changed all the time I was with Top Rank. People did think that, having a position in the public eye, I would be paid large amounts of money, but this was not so. Some of the youngsters who attended probably had more cash in their pockets than myself!

I now had my ally back with me for any future confrontations. The next three years would be very interesting. Back in the old routine, the weeks hardly varied. Our usual friends, the local groups, filled in many spots, Dadio and myself again joining them with the odd number. I still did Johnny Kidd's number *Shakin' All Over,* but now wearing his original eye patch.

The groups who generally tolerated our occasional melodious outbursts were Terry Sexton and The Shakes, Mick Sagar's Cresters, The Mel Clarke Four, and The Tornadoes. Amongst the professional groups we did numbers with were The Barron Knights, The Hollies, The Rocking Berries, The Mersey Beats, and Lee Walker and The Travellers. This last group were appearing at the Majestic, Hull, and Dadio and myself were asked to compere a package show with them. This we did for four weeks on a Saturday, travelling over in Dadio's old Ford Popular, pre-M62 days, and often foggy. But it was a change.

We did a similar thing with the Barron Knights, this time at the Winter Gardens, Morecambe. As we were not members of the group, people wondered who we were. Pete Langford of the Barron Knights introduced us as the Singing Top Rank DJs. After the numbers, my usual, and Dadio's *Whole Lot a' Shakin' Goin' on,* we were asked for encores. The Barron Knights graciously accepted and played through the numbers again. This was typical of the Barron Knights of that time, probably a way of thanking us for the many return bookings we instigated for them at the Gaumont and the Majestic.

The Barron Knights, one of the only big beat groups to score big hits with records specifically designed to be funny, were actually a

The Barron Knights. Our modest efforts helped them to the top. But we were soon forgotten!

band who could always deliver a different evening's entertainment far beyond the dictates of passing trends. At this time vocalist Duke d'Mond was emphasised in the billing as he was fundamentally a front. It was said that he was sensitive about his non-instrumental roll, as in publicity shots he often contrived to clutch a harmonica or other minor percussion instrument to counteract this impression. The others were; Barron Anthony (bass), Butch Baker (lead), and drummer Dave Bellinger. It was during one of their visits to the Majestic in 1963 that Pete Langford stated that, if they didn't make the big time in twelve months,

DUKE D'MOND *(Fontana Records)*

they would seriously consider packing it in. Ironically, the clincher came in July 1964 when the marathon *Call Up The Groups* marched onto Number Three after a sensational *Ready, Steady, Go* preview. They were on their way, having three more palpable hits, and well into the Eighties the Barron Knights were still popular.

The last time I saw them was in the late Sixties at the Batley Variety Club, and they just did not want to know! I felt like a "hanger-on". I was treated as though I was something that had just crawled out of the cheese. I had seen other people being used by pop stars and then behind their backs being spoken of with contempt. This was how I felt, and for all the years since I have had a resentment for the Barron Knights because of their attitude that night. They could laugh all the way to the bank because of people like Dal, Dadio, and the thousands of youngsters who paid their admissions to see them, and our modest efforts to obtain bookings for them must have helped to create a foothold to their success.

Two Bradford Majestic-ites pose in the latest fashion (1962) Diana & Jill.

CHAPTER SEVENTEEN

The List is Endless

During 1962/3 the only change to note with our established format was the moving of Mr Mitchell, who I believe made his way back to 'The Smoke'. Things had improved and for those last few months he had almost compensated for his earlier attitude by giving his blessing to the established Rock 'n' Roll nights and also forthcoming attractions. The new manager was Carl Glass, a young man, small in stature, who was to give us no grief and helped in the continuation of the future shows.

LEFT: Shane Fenton (Alvin Stardust) was easily recognised on our visit to 'Vivs' Bar'.
BELOW:Shane Fenton and the Fentones. An early practice session at home.

Shane Fenton (now Alvin Stardust) paid his first visit to us during that year, during the success of his minor hit *Five Foot Two, Eyes of Blue*. Although early days for Shane, you could see that he had that certain something that would take him far. On this visit, during the show I left Dadio on stage whilst Shane and myself slipped out to the Majestic Pub in Manchester Road (Viv's Bar). There were quite a few people in, some of them en-route to the dance. We were surrounded by glances, nudges "Is it or isn't it?" remarks. Shane bought me a pint and in no time at all we were back in the dance hall. To linger would have been unwise.

Kiki Dee outside Bradford's City Hall (1986) "... she would sometimes pay us a visit to join in the dancing."
(Courtesy *Telegraph & Argus*).

Kiki Dee was doing well at this time and she would sometimes pay us a visit to join in the dancing. On these occasions I would pass complimentary remarks over the mike, as a way of saying "local girl makes good".

Emile Ford and The Checkmates — actually the first coloured star to perform at the Majestic — left a pleasant memory with his Number One hit of 1959. It still remains one of the longest questions ever asked by a title on a single - *What Do You Want To Make Those Eyes At Me For?*

Emile Ford had a Number One hit in 1959 with 'What do you want to make those eyes at me for?'

Eden Kane. On his appearance at the Majestic he had to mime to his record - no mike!

Eden Kane followed with a rather mediocre performance which was not actually his fault as, just before he was due to sing his Number One hit *Well I ask you*, the PA system went on the blink. The evening ended with Dadio holding a microphone for him which was plugged into one of the backing group's amplifiers. I think the girls mainly remembered him for his good looks that evening rather than his performance. Later he did make other Top Ten hits which proved popular, namely *Get Lost, Forget Me Not,* and *I Don't Know Why.*

When British records made the UK charts in the early Sixties, it was usually with solo stars such as Marty Wilde and Billy Fury with their backing groups in identical stage outfits skulking behind the main spotlights. Occasionally, vocal or duo groups would put up a fight. One such duo was The Allisons who, on the strength of their popular hit *Are You Sure* in the European Song Contest, made television appearances and toured the country with their act. The only thing I remember of that Friday night show was John Allison accompanying me to Viv's Bar during the break but, unlike Shane Fenton, no-one enquired who he was.

THE ALLISONS on fontana RECORDS

Did the circuit tours on the strength of their popular hit in the Eurovision Song Contest 'Are You Sure?'

Our own local groups were still doing the circuits. New names were coming to the fore, some staying longer than others. Many of these played the Majestic, Gaumont, pubs and clubs, and many other venues around the old West Riding and beyond. Some dropped out in the early stages. Others survived through the Sixties, but only just, as drummers, guitarists and vocalists left to join other groups in the hope of making the big time. These groups supplemented the many weeks we had no stars booked, the usual format being Dal, Dadio and a local group. We were left again to our own devices, to run these shows just as we wished, with the compliments of Carl Glass, the manager. Thus it was up to ourselves whether we re-booked any of the groups. Having this power we could pick and choose. Any smart-Alec group who came along thinking they were chocolate were soon re-educated. Any re-booking would be determined on their attitude. Not to re-book anyone was quite a rare occasion, although three in particular do spring to mind and, for obvious reasons, I cannot name them.

No 1, a fairly new group who did lack experience, were booked without our knowledge and it was for the popular Friday night. To say they were flat was an understatement. Their average age was fourteen so, in their first half hour spot, I had to terminate their performance by drowning out their sound with a record, as I suspected the punters were uneasy and I had caught the odd shout of "Rubbish!" The floor was empty, nobody was dancing. There were over one thousand teenagers squaring for a riot. I had almost done my disappearing act down to Viv's but something told me not to. Wait and listen, which I did. I do not embarrass easily, but on this occasion I most certainly was. My experience was to offer applause for a skilful performance, but I was at a loss at what action to take for such an abysmal effort as this. But, as luck would have it, within seconds of returning to play a disc, the floor was heaving to the Twist. Our young hopefuls had absconded sharply to the dressing room, leaving myself and Dadio to entertain the troops for the whole of the evening. I think the manager paid them out of sympathy, but they left with the old adage of "Don't ring us, we'll ring you" resounding in their ears.

It was Carl who had booked this unheard of group over the phone, so from that date most of the local bookings were done by Dadio or myself.

No 2 group who were not asked to return was for a different matter. Some money went missing from somebody's coat pocket in Dressing Room 1. When the culprit was confronted he immediately owned up. Rather than involve the 'Bobbies' the group was blacklisted, but a year later the group was allowed to return to the Majestic again because the member had been dismissed by his fellow group members whose reputation he had dented because of his behaviour.

No 3 group's reason for extradition would today be termed as "they incited punch-ups". Guys with big mouths and chips on their shoulders to match. As a bunch of musicians they were quite good, but didn't they know it! Their nasty disposition left a lot to be desired. After jabbing me in the back with a bony index finger, shouting orders, a free-for-all ensued which did nobody any good. There were no winners that night.

Things on the whole were getting better, and for the next few months the real big time would come to the Majestic. These months would be the peak, anything after would definitely by a trough.

CHAPTER EIGHTEEN

''The'' Star

We all have our own definition of what makes a star. Many artistes I met and introduced were undoubtedly stars of that decade: big stars, household names, even of international fame. One of the first of these was Gene Vincent. Gene was to appear at the Majestic. To this day I cannot recall who booked him. This guy had been a favourite of mine from my army days, from the barrack rooms of Aldershot to the Crater district of Aden. His music accompanied my travels, his hit at the time being *Be-Bop-A-Lula*. It must have been special because even my mum could be heard humming along while doing the ironing. Not many mothers at that time were as square as we used to think. Gene Vincent had previously appeared in Bradford but that was at a Gaumont Theatre Package Show which was the first time I had seen him. I was impressed, but the majority of the audience were not, particularly during a number which was a favourite of his but obviously not of the fans, namely *Somewhere Over The Rainbow* sang, not as a rock number as you might have expected, but as a flowery ballad, which, of course, it was originally intended to be.

After five years in the Navy, Gene suffered a mishap that would alter the course of his life. While walking across the base, he was struck by a staff car which inflicted multiple fractures to his left leg. In later years when referring to his injury he would often attribute it to a motorcycle crash or bullet wound sustained in Korea.

Again in April 1960, he was involved in the same car accident which killed Eddie Cochran at Chippenham in Wiltshire. Eddie had just recorded the prophetically titled *Three Steps To Heaven*. It became his only Number One hit single the following June, thus becoming the second posthumous Number One in the British charts. This crash resulted in Gene receiving more injuries to the leg and pelvis which necessitated the use of callipers. Whether it was that Gene was using pain killing drugs to quell the pain that night at the Gaumont I am unsure, but I admit his performance was not up to standard. This did not tarnish my admiration for him, he was my hero.

Not so with the rest of the fans. The idiot brigade began to heckle and taunt, "Hop-along", etc. Poor Gene, groaning and sweating in his black leather gear, legs akimbo unable to conceal his metal calliper, he endured the insults bravely to the end. He departed the Gaumont stage with some applause from the loyal embarrassed section of fans as well as myself.

I used my usual Bilko-inspired excuses* for getting backstage to meet him, which was quite difficult on this occasion because of

---

* *Ernie Bilko, the fictional American army sergeant portrayed in a television series, who could talk his way into any situation.*

The *Star — Gene Vincent*

GAUMONT, Bradford TEL. 26716

Manager — J. S. C. PHILCOX

SATURDAY JANUARY 30th. 6 & 8.15 p.m.

LARRY PARNES PRESENTS | ONE NIGHT ONLY

The Two Sensational American Stars !
In person — First time ever in England.

GENE VINCENT | EDDIE COCHRAN

BACKED BY THE FABULOUS WILDCATS | HIT RECORDER of "C'mon Everybody" & "Summertime Blues."

VINCE EAGER

STAR OF TV, RADIO, STAGE & RECORDS, Plus

ALL STAR SUPPORTING COMPANY

TICKETS: 7/6, 6/6, 5/6, 5/-, 4/6 & 3/6.

Jan 1960: The following April Gene Vincent was severely injured in the same car crash that killed Eddie Cochran at Chippenham, Wiltshire.

the audience's reaction to his performance, resulting in their bad feelings for him being reciprocated. I won through and was ushered into his presence for about thirty seconds, during which he gave me a signed photograph from his album, but I did not savour the moment because of the tense atmosphere that surrounded the man himself and his manager. Therefore, it was not possible to expedite the many questions I wished to ask. I wished him well and left, little knowing that, in the not too distant future, I would have all the time in the world to ask him as many questions as I liked.

Now, two years later, he was to be our guest star at the Majestic. His backing group of the old days were The Bluecaps. On his tour round the UK our own Sounds Incorporated accompanied him, most of whom I knew from a previous visit to the Gaumont Ballroom in 1961. Monday night was the date. As usual I was at the Majestic in the afternoon, ensuring everything was in order. I could accomplish this by disappearing with the van from work on the pretence I was checking out a mislaid order, hence being able to spend some time getting the arrangements for the evening organised.

Sounds Incorporated were already well on the way to having set up all the equipment. Acknowledgements were exchanged and it was nice to be remembered by this very talented group. There would be only one live spot for our guest and that would be at 9 o'clock for 45 minutes. He would not be there in the afternoon, and would arrive about an hour before his performance. Needless to say, I was back down at the Majestic by 7 o'clock. The usual queue four deep wound its way crocodile-style down Morley Street and disappeared around the Alhambra corner. The usual catcalls greeted me as I walked up to the door. What with the publicity, I knew we would have a capacity of nearly 1,200 people. I wandered down to the dressing room to change. The group were tuning up on stage, so, on reaching the dressing room I was confronted by Gene Vincent himself, perched on a chair sipping a Coke. "Gene Vincent, I'm Dal Stevens, the DJ here at the Majestic". Waiting for him to answer, I fully anticipated a sharp rebuke or put down. This was not to be. Just as I hoped, he was a real gentleman. We chatted amicably for the next fifteen minutes. Who would have thought five years ago, as I sat watching him in the Jayne Mansfield film *The Girl Can't Help It* that I would be sat conversing with him face to face. He was a little fatter in the face than he had been during our first encounter, but there was the same enigmatic quality about him. He had very curly black hair and, in keeping with most of the American stars of that time, sported a permanent suntan. It's funny that most of the American stars that I met all seemed to possess good manners. Gene was actually calling me "Sir", but by the early hours of the morning this was to change to Dal.

My colleague Dadio came on the scene and was treated likewise. The show was a tremendous success. Gene did his spot until 10 o'clock, one sweet hour of *Shake, Rattle and Roll* adorned in black leather jacket and trousers. Needless to say, I did not pop down to Viv's for a swift half, as I wished to relish the moment.

Curiosity, they say, killed the cat. This nearly happened to me. Later that evening, during the end of his performance, I went down to his dressing room to see if all was at peace. The room was dark and empty. Putting on the light, I glanced upon his open case abounding with dirty socks, crumpled shirts, etc. Yes, the stars are just like the rest of us under the charisma. My eyes registered on a letter with a photograph attached which was protruding from the side of his case. I furtively picked it up and began reading. It was from an English girl from London, declaring her love for him. Her name was Julie and I think she must have been his current girlfriend of the time. I felt quite a heel, but managed to convince myself that I wasn't doing any harm. In hindsight it would have been better if I had taken a pair if his dirty socks and kept them for today's pop star memorabilia auctions — could have made a fortune — but then I would probably have had difficulty authenticating them. So, I left everything as I had found it. As I had introduced him onto the stage through the courtesy of Sounds Incorporated, Dadio brought him off, amongst the rousing applause of many hundreds of teenagers crowding round the front of the stage — these had been moments of listening not dancing. The group then left the stage and Dadio and myself finished off the last half hour. Although it was the "follow that" situation that prevailed again, as it was with Joe Brown, Gene Vincent had to run the gauntlet to the dressing room much slower in his case because of his incapacity with his legs. The crowd had built up around the door, many with autograph books. It was then, while we were finishing off, that we had to take piles of these books down to Gene to sign. "No problem, happy to do so" was Gene's reply.

It was nearly 11.30 pm before the area was cleared enough for him to leave. Thinking he would be accommodated at the Midland or Victoria, I was surprised to find out that he and Sounds Incorporated were booked into the Castle Hotel at the top of Albion Street, off Westgate. Coincidental because the company I worked for was situated twenty yards away from there, just around the corner. Dadio and myself were asked if we would like to join them for a drink, so we all went up to the Castle. With glasses charged we passed the time away exchanging experiences of the pop scene. Only one or two residents were in. It was late and, to this day, I cannot remember if drinking was permitted at that hour. I only know that the bar was open and the management cordially served drinks upon request.

During our conversation I remember an old gentleman sitting on a stool at the side of the bar asking me who the "Yank" was. "Gene Vincent" I retorted, "The American pop star", my voice trembling with humility. "Oh" was the reply, as he quickly re-adjusted his glasses and returned to reading a racing form paper.

Around 1.30 am the little group was down to Gene Vincent, Barry Cameron, Alan Holmes, of Sounds Incorporated, Dadio and myself. I was sat on a stool next to Gene Vincent. The topic of girls emerged and he began to tell us of this girl he had known for some time, an English girl from London. "Oh, Julie" I said nonchalently. Gene looked up and, bursting with curiosity, said "How the hell do you know her name is Julie, even the Sounds don't know that?". "Well," I said, "When I first met you earlier down in the dressing room, you were reading a letter, and I could see on the back of it, 'Love Julie'." "Jesus," he said, "I should be more careful." I don't know why he wanted to keep the name a secret but I hoped he would forget about it as I feared that, if he studied the incident in depth, he would recall that he was reading the *Telegraph & Argus* when we first met. I quickly changed the subject. I entertained him with one of my old party tricks which consisted of breaking a pencil in half with an old one pound note. Many pencils were broken during the early hours of that morning. This had Gene fascinated, how could a folded paper pound note hit a pencil held by someone and break it clean in half. This trick I performed many times, with Gene pleading with me to explain how it was done. Somehow I never got round to telling him.

In the early hours of that morning I said my farewell to a great star. We did meet again some two years later. He was in a package show of which he was just one of the many stars in the lower order. His last words to me were "Hey, Dal, you never did show me how to do that pencil trick". Ravages of time, car and motorcycle accidents all took their toll. After a few years of sliding down the scale he was just climbing back up when Mr "Be-Bop-A-Lula" Gene Vincent died of heart failure in 1971.

CHAPTER NINETEEN
Package Shows

While the Majestic was enjoying what would be its best era, the other big Rock 'n' Roll venues at the Gaumont Theatre were doing the same. These were the so-called Package Shows where as many as five or six top line performers would be on the same show. In my capacity as Bradford's Number One DJ (certain competitors might not agree!), I had easy access to these shows, which meant I was free to wander around backstage and meet the stars. Managers of these stars had police-like protection over their proteges. I have seen certain people, who have managed to avoid security, being frogmarched and literally thrown out of the theatre for being backstage.

One such person was a friend, and fellow DJ, who was in the habit of always being where he was not wanted. We all had to admit that he was not easily deterred and could be found at most venues to the fore, or in the background. This night in particular (the show featuring Del Shannon), he was being frogmarched by two burly Kray twins look-alikes. He passed me with a forlorn look of anguish on his face, which almost prompted me to intercede, but I knew he would not have done it for me, so I just turned a blind eye.

The vast Gaumont arena. Ideal for "package" shows.

Phil and Don Everly. They gave me a five minute interview.

It was at one of these shows that I met the Everly Brothers, Don and Phil. I was only allowed five minutes of their time, and they kindly signed the programme for me. Our conversation consisted of general chit-chat. On the same bill was Mark Wynter (another Eden Kane type), never

The Package Show. Buddy Holly appeared at the Gaumont a few months before his death.

really Number One material, but dependable for this type of show and the odd television spot. A smoothie for the girls, he was bounding up and down the back-stage stairs like a bubble in a bottle, when I asked him for his autograph. Lulu was just coming out of the side dressing room on the same show, sweet sixteen and backed by her group The Luvvers. She was just beginning to make it with the ashtray-rasp voice that pushed her up in the Top Twenty stakes to Number 7 with *Shout*. These days she looks remarkably young, in fact, she looks younger now than she did when I met her all those years ago with a beehive hairdo. She also had a rather spotty face.

Likewise, meeting Billy Fury on the same venue. "Sad Face Fury" some other pop star once remarked. He did have that tragic 'James Dean' look and the same certain characteristics, but there the similarities ended, although in the Sixties he was asked to moderate his sub-Presley gyrations! When Billy died a few years ago, Yorkshire Television's *Calendar* paid a nice tribute to him by ending the programme with him singing *Maybe Tomorrow*. I would have been surprised if it didn't bring a few of the old Gaumont and Majestic girls to tears had they seen it.

During the Del Shannon package show I was standing just offstage in the wings behind the curtain. On finishing his act he ran off the stage towards me and said "Shall I go back for an encore?". I said "Yes", pushing him off to the centre of the stage. This happened three times and we had never even met. Later, it transpired, he thought I was the stage manager and, while it was accepted that he would do an encore, the well mannered American was

Billy Fury played at the Gaumont.

DEL SHANNON *London Records*

"Shall I go back for an encore?" he asked. Even the DJ's mum gets an autograph!

asking if it was OK. Later we did meet and I was asked, along with two girlfriends of his, to a late press supper at the Victoria Hotel. Again, a firm friendship was set up. This was because he was an avid 78s record collector. He asked if I could obtain some certain old records. I was able to furnish him with these over the time he was on tour, which resulted in him contacting me by 'phone or letter over the years in the pursuit of such records. He was a good Rock innovator who built up a successful four year chart career on the strength on *Runaway* — his only Number One hit. Del Shannon was very active again up until his death in January 1990. He was 51. His letters and autographs to me were misplaced some years ago, the only autograph I have now is the one he gave to my mother when he visited my home during a later UK tour.

My Boy Lollipop. The star of this hit number was a young West Indian girl called "Millie". She was on a small package show at the Gaumont and, in my usual capacity backstage, I had the pleasure of meeting this delightful young lady. While being chaperoned by both her manager and family,

'My Boy Lollipop' Millie took me out on a date: lunch and Cartwright Hall!!

she also had a certain amount of freedom in as much as she asked me out to lunch the next day as it was a two day stop-over. This was actually the first time I had been taken out on a date and been paid for!

She was particularly proud of a large gold bracelet given to her by the president of the group of islands from where she came. In the centre of the bracelet was an enormous pearl about one inch across, probably worth a small fortune by now. The next day I joined her at the Victoria for lunch, then escorted her around Lister Park and Cartwright Hall. A dainty kiss on the cheek brought this rather sweet episode to a close, but weeks later I received a huge envelope containing a mass of photographs all autographed "With all my love".

Little Richard. Tore off his shirt and threw it to the audience.

Perhaps one of the best shows I can remember was Little Richard's visit to the Gaumont Theatre. His backing group was led by the phenomenal Bo Diddley, who was a star in his own right. On this occasion Little Richard, perspiring profusely, tore off his shirt and threw it to the audience. I met him later in the evening and, like all those moments I look back on, I wished I'd had a camera to record those precious moments, but I came away from that encounter with a super autograph inscribed "To Dale, A Very Nice Guy, God Bless", along with his address and a request to contact him if I needed any help regarding any DJ work in the States. I had mentioned during the conversation that my ambition was to be a DJ Stateside. So, whilst I had three full nights of disc jockeying with my colleague Dadio, the other nights were occupied fraternising with the stars at other venues. Meanwhile, back at the ranch . . . . .

To Dale
A Very Nice Guy
God bles
Little Richard
39 31 Manchester Place
Rive Side, Calif.

The autograph from Little Richard. I was to contact him if I required DJ work in the States.

CHAPTER TWENTY

The Best Years

From mid-1963 to early 1965, the Majestic had its best years for star attractions. This was mainly due to the forward planning of the manager Carl Glass. Unfortunately this would change later due to the appointment of other managers who thought that all the world revolved around Bingo. Dadio and myself had established ourselves as a good DJ team, working together on the stand or singularly. I think, by and large, we commanded much respect from the many hundreds of teenagers who came to our three established shows on Monday, Wednesday and Friday. Many of these people were now friends and it was difficult to visit Bradford on Saturday without being challenged by the odd fan. Fashions had changed to Italian style suits and Winklepickers which had taken the place of Teddy Jackets and thick crepe beetle-crusher shoes, although Radar and his Solo Bop clan would cling to this fashion well into the future.

The centre of Bradford also had begun to change. Buildings seemingly disappeared overnight, courting alleyways and snickets which had abounded in the city centre were lost. So new hideaways had to be found away from the new bright neon lights. More and more cinemas were closing or being used for Bingo. Many of the previously mentioned dance halls, with their resident bands, were also closing. Changes were sweeping through the City fast, making choices limited, whereas before, they were taken for granted. Competition was becoming less and people from nearby towns joined our locals, as they had nothing to compete with the Majestic and the stars we had to offer.

One similar successful venture was the Mecca on Manningham Lane, built on the old site of the skating rink. This modern building, with its starlight ceiling, was to offer some competition, especially on their Rock 'n' Roll night which was Monday, clashing with ours. At this time it was managed by Alan Boyce who, on my visits, would always greet me, the opposition, with a smile and jovial conversation. The other nights were devoted to Bingo, dance bands, and local firms' annual dances. They also had their star visitors. I remember seeing groups like The Temperance Seven and The Searchers, augmented by their DJ Mervin Wood who was a very good DJ. When I was in the dance hall he would always mention the fact, one time inviting me onto his DJ stand to play a few discs, much to the delight of some of the Majestic-ites who would be visiting the opposition that night.

At that time we were holding our own with Mecca competition. We had plenty of publicity in the *Telegraph & Argus* regarding forthcoming attractions, so keeping the three nights going along very well. Like the Mecca, other nights were Bingo, and Saturday night was still Billy Hey's Dance Orchestra. During this time, when the holidays came around we would ask Carl Gresham to take over for two weeks. By the end of the fortnight the fans would welcome us back with open arms, not that they did not like Carl, but he had a style of his own which was not necessarily ours. Later on he was to leave us all behind to develop his own style, making him a very popular DJ on local radio. But, thanks to him, we could go away knowing the shop was in capable hands.

During this time I also changed my job and took a career with a firm of assurance brokers. The intellectual by day and the DJ at night! This was also helpful in that I had a company car which meant I would no longer need to face the prospect of running for buses.

Things were going great, but unfortunately the euphoria was not to last, as the final few chapters will illustrate.

CHAPTER TWENTY ONE
Nostalgia At Its Best

From the 1960s the heavyweights of pop comedy were Freddie and The Dreamers. This Manchester group, whose earlier comedy routine included trouser dropping, sketches, slapstick, and amateur acrobatics, were blended together playing the clubs in Hamburg, where Freddie's catchphrase "Just a minute" originated. A hybrid of Frank Spencer and Buddy Holly, he was once described as a sort of pop star you wouldn't mind your girlfriend admiring.

In 1963, after a smattering of TV appearances , and then a *Thank Your Lucky Stars* spot featuring *If You Gotta Make A Fool Of Somebody*, he was up to Number Three, followed by *I'm Telling You Now*, which went to Number Two. With that, Freddie and The Dreamers were established. With all this behind him, frantic Freddie appeared at the Majestic. His night was on the Friday. The show itself was a television copy. Most groups, when seen live, are completely different to their television performance. Not so Freddie and his Dreamers. The usual build up was observed by bouncers and staff. The long settees were placed strategically round the stage to hinder any would-be chancer who might like to try their luck. A policeman would be on duty to curtail any idiot amongst the one thousand two hundred teenagers, you always got one or two, but one policeman was sufficient. You would need a squad of policemen these days!

The usual arrangements had been made regarding introductions. This being my turn, we were all ready. We had previously met and chatted: "How do you wish to be introduced?" etc. No problems were created by Freddie, he had the professional sense to leave it to us.

This was one of the few occasions I went for a drink before the show, not that I needed it, nor did Derek Quinn, lead guitarist of the Dreamers. But, on fancying a pint we nipped out through the rear door and into Morley Street, and across Great Horton Road to the Alexander Bar. Freddie had decided to join us, but on opening the rear door we were confronted by part of the queue which had wound its way down from the entrance to the Alhambra, then all the way up Morley Street to the other side of the Majestic building. I cannot remember the size of that queue being equalled. So, Freddie had to do an about turn. Had he taken a chance and run for it, he wouldn't have got back in. Derek Quinn was not recognised, so we got safely across into the bar.

At 9 o'clock everything was ready for Freddie's one hour spot. My so-called introduction was drowned by one thousand two hundred screaming voices. With a leap and a bound Freddie jack-knifed onto the stage with his Top Twenty Hit *I'm Telling You Now* inserting his catchphrase of "Just a minute" here and there. He had the packed Majestic enthralled for sixty minutes of non-stop entertainment.

For one incredible moment, The Beatles apart, Freddie Garrety ruled British pop. A good night was had by all. The reflection was shown in the *Telegraph & Argus* the following day.

The Merseybeats were another group from that other county who graced the Majestic with their presence during our best years. With appearances at The Cavern and toughened during the required Hamburg stretch, their local standing became such that they were rated tenth in the Mersey hierachy of groups. Their dress was a change from the macho leathers and Burton lounge suits. Their preference being frilly shirts and bolero jackets. Some

Freddie had to do a quick U-turn when he saw the crowd outside. But Derek Quinn and myself made it across the road to the Alex Bar for a quick drink.

THE MERSEYBEATS

Their frilly shirts and bolero jackets were a change from macho leathers and Burton lounge suits.

accusations of "Nancy Boys" were heard, but the Merseybeats certainly made the girls scream at the Majestic that Monday night. Their rendition of *Wishin' and Hopin'* being their popular number at that time.

Billie Davis. All change: one for the boys.

Mike Sarne with Wendy Richards made a brief appearance one Wednesday evening, and performed their Number One hit *Come Outside*. This was the saga of an optimistic boy at a Saturday night dance trying to persuade his date to step out into the moonlight with him. The number went down very well, but, to fill the rest of the time in with nonentities did not work, and I believe the tour did not last to its full extent. Mike Sarne went on to do a follow up, this time with Billie Davis called *Will I What?* and other less original variations on the theme.

Billie Davis was actually the only female vocalist we booked for an evening. Such a change from all the groups and male pop stars. Already known for the voice-off for Mike Sarne's *Will I What?*, she went on to make the odd pop record. This, and her Top Twenty hit, a Lulu-type bouncy number called *I Know Something About Love,* was quite a change — one for the boys! She had a backing group whose name evades me, but she left a pleasant memory of quite a nice girl, although the remarks some of her teenage peers were making were not complimentary. The mutterings under their breath, and behind cupped hands, were not quite polite coming from ladies, but she was definitely appreciated by the lads.

A further Liverpool product again invaded the Majestic, namely The Fourmost. Originally they were called The Four Jays (remember Dal Stevens and the Blue Jays?), until Brian Epstein changed it to the more symmetrical Fourmost. This group started in The Cavern with "take-offs" of Cliff, the Vernon Girls, The Goons, and many others. This lead them to an eight month run with Cilla Black at the London Palladium, and Top Twenty hits like *Little Girl,* and *I'm In Love.* Their biggest smash hit, by which they are best remembered, is *A Little Loving.* The group performed well at the Majestic, interacting with bouts of their earlier comedy talents. Nothing really unusual about the group, but they did possess a wealth of talent.

Another comedy group that came to our Friday night packed house were one of the most credible of all the bands who ended up in variety: The Rocking Berries. After successive hits with *He's In Town* and *Poor Man's Soul,* and the UK tour supporting P J Proby, the usual stint of dance hall venues now took place. The instrumental numbers went down particularly well that night, as it was one of the few groups that could give a continuous Rock 'n' Roll beat.

Billy J Kramer and The Dakotas entourage joined us for renderings of his Number One hits *Little Children* and *Bad to Me* and his other less popular hits *Do You Want To Know A Secret* and *I'll Keep You Satisfied.* For some time now their numbers were part of our popular requests, so it was quite an occasion to see many of the audience dance to a live performance. I remember Billy J was not a hit with Dadio or myself. He was good, a true professional, and he knew it. He did not have much to say to us, our conversation could have been written on the back of a postage stamp. I wonder if it could have been perhaps because I mentioned to one of his group during a practice in the afternoon that his voice sounded a little trembly. Listen next time someone plays one of his 45s.

It was while we were enjoying this "Top of The Pops" highlight in Bradford that we heard the news that Carl Glass, the temporary manager of twelve months, was to move. It was a sad occasion for us, though I doubt many people reading this will remember him. But he took over from Mitchell at a bad time and helped to bring the Majestic back into the limelight, with a name, well-known in the North and South as a venue for the touring top groups. Hopefully, someone of his ilk would replace him and maintain the success he had brought to the Majestic.

CHAPTER TWENTY TWO
The Iceman Cometh

I think that both Dadio and myself knew on our first meeting with the new manager that we would not be compatible. From Nottingham, Mr Harry Radley entered our domain, a tall slim man in his early forties with swept back greying wavy hair. Within two weeks his hair style was to change, drastically brought about by a visit to Mario's. The new image was close cropped, not unlike Nero, who we were sure he was trying to emulate. His rather officious patronising manner soon had our backs up, especially as he made it clear from the start that Bingo was his main interest. I put this down on paper because not many of our friends would have realised at the time why we went from the sublime to the ridiculous. One thing we noticed about our fearless leader was that, if there was any publicity as a result of our popularity, he would be there in the limelight to take the credit. We had contracted stars for future bookings through the foresight of Carl Glass, so hopefully we would have a continuation of our success. As previously mentioned, we purchased our records from Woods of Sunbridge Road, but once again, as in the days of Mitchell, the number of records we could buy was greatly reduced. We argued our point, but to no avail. The restriction on records brought resentment from the teenagers who still made requests and expected us to be able to play the latest discs, especially those in the Top Twenty. You can imagine our embarrassment once again, on being asked to play something from the top of the hit parade, and having to explain why we didn't have it. So Dadio and myself became the whipping boys and took the caustic comments from our frustrated patrons. The retort made when we said we didn't have such a record was that "Well they have it at the Mecca". Actually some did help by bringing records from home.

Completely demoralised we asked for a rise, we had nothing to lose. This exercise got us nowhere, only a curt enquiry as to whether one of us could manage each show. We were still only being paid £1.10 shillings each for each night. In fact our request rebounded back on us as, within a week we had been contacted by the Inland Revenue, the conclusion being that as we had not been paying tax on our DJ earnings, we would have to repay at 2/6 (12½p) per week. I remember paying that sum for two years.

Another transgression was the performers royalty sheets which had not been filled in by the management, advising how many times a record was played. This number was accumulated throughout the UK and the said performer and record label would get a percentage sum for the use of the disc, that is royalties. So this was another of his suggestions we had to adhere to.

In spite of all this aggravation the shows were going well: Dal, Dadio and the local groups, plus stars. Thanks to Carl Glass the stars and semi-stars came and went. The London group, The Bow Street Runners, who were winners of a *Ready, Steady, Go* contest, appeared briefly. They looked more like primary school teachers than pop stars. The Four Pennies cashed in at the Majestic on Monday evening. Originating from Blackburn this time, they played a lot of Everly Brothers' material, plus the Number One hit of 1964 *Juliet*. Cliff Bennett was back with us, also the Flintstones, and as previously stated, the Barron Knights. A change from the usual came in the form of the Honeycombs; different because the drummer was a girl, Ann "Honey" Lantree. They were not the first all male band with a girl drummer, but it was the first for us. With a one-off Number One hit *Have I The Right* they, like others, were doing the circuits. They proved to be popular at the Majestic, especially as their Number One hit had always been a favourite to dance to. The Fortunes paid a visit well before their Number Two hit *You've Got Your Troubles* and the later hit *Here It Comes Again*. These were just a handful of the many who passed through.

Gerry and The Pacemakers. Gerry certainly hadn't much to smile about that night!

Of the top stars, Gerry and The Pacemakers created an eventful evening. As they were a top group I made my usual late afternoon call to see if they had arrived. This time no group, nothing. I put out the DJ equipment (not the records, these tended to walk) and went home to change. On our arrival at 7 o'clock Dadio and myself were welcomed by the manager. He said he was glad we had arrived, he fussed about us to the point of being obsequious. The reason for his most uncharacteristic approach unfurled in minutes when he informed us that Gerry and The Pacemakers had arrived but with no equipment, instruments etc. Was there anything we could do to resolve the problem? We set off down to the dressing room and encountered Gerry Marsden. Had he any ideas? we said, " ...... off" he said. This obscenity was directed at two ex-soldiers by an ex-choirboy. It transpired that the van bringing the instruments from Torquay had broken down near Manchester and would not have a hope in hell of getting to Bradford in time for the show. After calming Mr Marsden down we asked what equipment and instruments they would need. He furnished us with the details and, with Gerry's drumming brother Fred in tow, we headed back to the manager's office to see what we could do. Thanks to our relationships with the local groups we were able to contact Terry Sexton and the Telecasters, also

Geoff and the Fairlanes from Shipley. Typically, both groups responded to the SOS and, like the troupers they were, and in their own time, they supplied Gerry and The Pacemakers with their own equipment and instruments. In the meantime, with the usual attendance expected, Dadio and I got the show on the road. We controlled the bewildered crowd that night (as they could see no equipment on stage) right up until 9.15pm when Gerry and The Pacemakers took to the stage. Things were running very late because, as well as the mix-up earlier when the equipment finally arrived, they had to practice a little while on their new instruments down in the dressing rooms. Looking at the write-up in the *Telegraph & Argus* the next day you would have thought Dadio and myself didn't exist, thanks to Radley's observations. He was the hero and saved the day; we did not get a mention! Thanks were made to us later that evening by Gerry, and also to our local groups for their help. Mr Radley was nowhere around, probably in his office being interviewed by the said newspaper (see cutting).

Pop group had no instruments

TOP pop group Gerry and the Pacemakers came to Bradford last night and nearly found themselves in the middle of a riot. For Gerry was there, the Pacemakers were there—but no instruments were there.

And Mr. Harry Radley, manager of the Majestic Ballroom, where Gerry and his boys were billed as the top attraction at a teenage dance, peeped cautiously out of his office at 1,100 milling youngsters, and shuddered.

The driver of the van bringing the Pacemakers' instruments from Torquay had just rung to say that he had broken down outside Manchester and couldn't get to Bradford in time.

"I had the makings of a full scale riot on my hands," said Mr. Radley today. "The group wouldn't have been able to perform and the kids would have torn the place apart."

The night was saved by two local groups—Geoff and the Fairlanes, from Shipley, and Terry Sexton and the Telecasters, of Bradford. Mr. Radley rang each of them. They came round and lent the Pacemakers their own instruments— two guitars, a bass guitar and a set of drums, plus amplifying equipment.

Gerry and the Pacemakers, the lads from Liverpool who top the hit parade—or thereabouts— were able to perform their latest hits to delighted squeals from the teenagers.

Around this time we had a special Rock 'n' Roll night celebrating Dal and Dadio's 1,000th record spin, which generated some publicity. A huge cake was made and presented to us on stage by none other than Harry Radley. We in turn presented the cake to the Children's Hospital in Bradford. The photograph in the *Telegraph & Argus* showed Dal and Dadio at the hospital and, of course, Mr Radley.

Not even a mention in Despatches!

ABOVE: Big cake donation to the Bradford Children's Hospital to mark our 1,000th Spinning Anniversary.

LEFT: A cutting from the Telegraph & Argus.

1000th. SPINNING ANNIVERSARY

THE Majestic Ballroom, Bradford, this week celebrated its 1,000th disc jockey session. Three nights a week, the resident D.J.'s, Del and Daddio spin the tops in pops.

Del is the name adopted by Derek Lister, a representative, who has been resident at the ballroom for the past three years. Derek lives at Ruffeild Street, Wyke, Bradford.

Daddio is the cool title taken by his friend, Terry Moran, a brewer's mechanic of Bright-Street, Bradford.

Just over three years ago both boys were hoping to make records— Derek with his own group and Terry with one of Bradford's best rock groups, the Dingoes, but their minds turned to introducing records rather than making them.

They still try a number or two now and again with visiting groups and say they enjoy it. Relaxation for them is spent in—playing more pop records!

Top liners

The Majestic has many top line groups booked to appear at their Monday, Wednesday, Friday evening Teenbeat Sessions. Freddie and The Dreamers are to play on Friday, October 4, and a package show featuring Shane Fenton and his group on Wednesday, October 9.

Next Wednesday—September 25— —the grand finals of the Bradford Rock Group Competition will be held. Since April about 20 groups have taken part in the competition, and hoping to win first prize—£25 —will be The Telecasters and Chad Wayne and The Chessmen.

CHAPTER TWENTY THREE
End of An Era

As all this was taking place, the Saturday Dance Band date came to an end. This popular venue for the older youth of the city was to close and be replaced by Bingo. Billy Hey, his Orchestra and his vocalist Jack, would be no more, to disappear, after giving many years of pleasure to the other side — the ballroom dancer. As previously stated, our new manager was Bingo-orientated. So what next? It was not long in coming. Our teenage Wednesday night was to be axed, again for Bingo. This we accepted as Wednesday was not always well attended. Sometimes we didn't have a local group on Wednesday because, being a mid-week venue, it wasn't always popular. Terry, alias Dadio, could also see that things were not to be the same so, with some reluctance, he departed. Like myself he had made many friends during his time as a DJ, both at the Gaumont earlier and latterly at the Majestic. With the Wednesdays now defunct, he finished off his final show with me one Friday evening. I remember he gave a little speech in his dulcet Brian Matthew's tones. For once the Hall was silent as he said his goodbyes. He was going but would not be forgotten.

So, I was back on my own, still with two successful nights, Monday and Friday. Mr Radley's next step was to cut down on advertising. The format in the *Telegraph & Argus* was drastically cut, so it was up to me to do as much advertising as I could during the show. It goes without saying that the most popular requests were for The Beatles records, a group, I hasten to add, we did not have at the Majestic. Likewise, The Dave Clark Five, The Kinks, The Searchers, The Stones, Manfred Mann. For this particular period these top stars dominated the Top Twenty with the occasional single vocalist ballad popping in at Number One for the odd week, for example, Sandie Shaw, Ken Dodd, Dusty Springfield. Some, like The Beachboys, were ideal for dancing to, but the other slow ballad types were not, but were played from time to time for smoochers.

The last of the really great groups to appear were The Hollies, so named as a tribute to Buddy Holly. This group, although around for some time (originally called The Deltas) had not made it to the top, *Just Like Me* only reaching Number Twenty Five, but then went on to score more UK single chart entries than any other group between 1963-1970. So, when a treatment of *Just One Look* almost topped the charts in 1964, The Hollies were established. This, and their Number One hit *I'm Alive*, gave them the status they had strived for. Nothing would ever be recorded in their biography that their visit to the Majestic was a particularly momentus occasion, but to myself, and the teenagers of Bradford of that time, it would be. It was a scoop, a real privilege to have them at the Majestic while their hit *Here I Go Again* was still in the Top Twenty.

I met The Hollies in the afternoon as they were set-

Dal & Dadio 1965. Two redundant DJs.

THE HOLLIES

Wilson Entertainment Agency.   TEMple Bar 3948

The Hollies. Almost the end of an era for the Majestic:
one of the last top groups to appear.
A kiss and a box of chocolates for the birthday girl
Diana from Tony Hicks.

ting up their equipment, spending most of the time conversing with Tony Hicks, the Peter Pan of the group. While talking I took a 'phone call from my future wife, Diana. Tony was standing by while I chatted. I mentioned this to Diana and, as it was her birthday that day, he wished her many happy returns over the 'phone. Later he enquired whether she was coming to the show that night. Alan Clark had joined us by now, so the three of us went across to Seabrooks Fish Restaurant down Great Horton Road. Passing the Olympus Coffee Bar I thought would be a problem, but we were only challenged by a girl in the doorway who shouted "Hi Dal". She didn't give a second glance to Tony Hicks or Alan Clarke. As all the youth of Bradford knew that The Hollies were appearing at the Majestic that night I could never understand how they passed by unrecognised down Great Horton Road.

The trip back was just the opposite. Word had got around, starting with the waitresses at Seabrooks. I can understand why some stars get annoyed by being approached by fans, but it is the price to pay for being famous. In the end we finished the meal in a staff room at Seabrooks. Being Northerners they certainly liked their fish and chips.

That night's performance was one to remember. As stated, I was now on my own, so I had to play the records and introduce The Hollies. No problem, but hard work. A worthy top group to conclude with, as nobody could compete with them on their performance that night. I was always one to relish moments like this because I knew these times would never come again. I can distinctly remember spending over an hour talking to the Hollies when they were packing their instruments and equipment away. Diana was with me and I introduced her to Tony Hicks. Tony said "Ah yes, the Birthday Girl". He gave her a kiss on the cheek and produced a large box of chocolates tied with a pink ribbon, together with a pretty card. You can imagine her delight and surprise. I have never been able to convince her that I did not put him up to it. I found out later that Sandy (the bouncer) had been sent out on the errand to buy these earlier in the afternoon.

The next Rock 'n' Roll night to bite the dust was Monday. My standing as Bradford's local DJ was being pruned drastically, with Radley playing the part of the ruthless gardener with no remorse shown. "The people are wanting more Bingo", he said. "Top Rank Bingo, that's where the money is". With Wednesday and Monday now gone, Friday night was the sad remainder. What price loyalty to the many Majestic fans who had stuck with us over the years? Their contempt was shown by their drift to the Mecca. We did nothing to hold them, there was no attempt to halt the Mecca-bound fans. Few records, no publicity, no top stars. Over the past two years the Majestic had gained in popularity throughout Bradford and district. It also had a quite prestigious reputation in the pop industry as a venue to the many pop groups and stars. I continued as best I could under the circumstances, watching the once energy-bounding crowd thin out, but with the loyal few still coming along, although I knew that their Monday evening's entertainment was at the Mecca. Our Fridays were brightened occasionally by the odd middle-of-the-road groups such as Dave Berry and The Cruisers playing hits like *Memphis, My Baby Left Me,* and *The Crying Game.* Groups like Dave Berry helped fill the Majestic on those Fridays but not to the capacity it had known. Needless to say, there was nothing worth preserving during those last months, and the Fridays would soon meet the same fate to make way for Bingo-mania. I did not wait for that as I left the Majestic in 1965. I did have the decency to pass over to a young teenager called Dave the workings of the DJ equipment, but the heart had dropped out of the Majestic. The pop scene and the styles of songs were also changing. The songs that explored the ups and downs of teenage romance sung by The Tabs, Frankies and Bobbies were on the decline. This type of star was now making a career in the numerous Sixties beach party movies. Most of them were performers to whom teen music was simply a means to an end, a pad from which to launch a career as a cabaret entertainer or film star. The worst of them were no more than puppets, told what to sing and how to sing it by world-wise managers, who had more than a hint of sharp practice about them.

There was also a feeling during the Summer of 1963 that The Beatles were offering something fresh. They reflected and inspired a new mood among a nation's youth that had its roots in a growing economic independence. By the end of 1964, The Beatles were already moving into new musical waters and challenging others to follow them. British pop was already beginning to change in character and content. More young R & B groups were coming to the fore, less interested in playing our Rock 'n' Roll dance music, to make what amounted to anti-establishment statements. They took their music seriously. A beat group could move from dance halls to seaside shows but, for R & B bands, this represented the worst kind of sell out. While our friends The Hollies would wreath themselves in smiles and suits in their quest for acceptance, the Rolling Stones deliberately cultivated an anti-social image with their sneers, scruffy clothes, and long unkempt hair. Looking back, I left at the end of an era. Mod style and Mod music would take over for a couple of years, this in turn being taken over by pop art progressing to psychedelically painted trucks, long hair, drugs, Flower Power and hippies.

A few DJ spots did come my way in the form of The

Dungeon in Westgate, with its blacked out windows, and a stint for Garth Cawood at the Top Twenty Club in Idle, plus the Victoria Hall at Keighley, where I kept in touch with my old friends from the local groups, not to mention the many ex-Majestic-ites.

The Majestic Dance Hall has now been swallowed up by the Alhambra extension and the young budding actors and dancers go through their paces unaware that they are treading the same boards as the vibrant, colourful Bradford youth of the Sixties. The place where their hopes, fears and ambitions were expressed as they danced away the laughter filled hours, many to meet their future partner there. When the Majestic was filled to capacity, the atmosphere was exhilarating, and I am proud that I was privileged to be part of it. I hope I have jogged a few memories, some happy, maybe some sad. It was a piece of the history of Bradford's youth in the Sixties. It was a time we will not forget while we are able to refer to the pages of Dal's memoirs.

STOP PRESS!
In 1991 Eric's missing trumpet (see page 28) was found in Duane's attic!!

Emile Ford • Tornados • Ricky Valance

Mike Sarne & Wendy Richards • Jet Harris & Tony Meeham

Gerry and the Pacemakers • Brian Poole and the Tremeloes

Billy J Kramer and The Dakotas

The Honeycombs • The Hollies • The Viscounts

The Yardbirds • Screaming Lord Sutch • The Flintstones

Sounds Incorporated • Zoot Money and His Big Roll Band

The Spotnicks • Barron Knights • The Rocking Berries

The Fourmost • The Karl Denver Trio • Jimmy Crawford

Freddie Starr and The Midnighters

Nero and The Gadiators • Dickie Pride

Freddie and The Dreamers

Jess Conrad • Heinz • Billie Davis

Wee Willie Harris • Vince Eager

The Allisons • Shane Fenton and The Fentones

Joe Brown and The Bruvvers

Cliff Bennett and The Rebel Rousers • The Fortunes

Dave Berry and The Cruisers

Danny Rivers and The River Men • The Four Pennies

The Merseybeats • The Swinging Blue Jeans

The Bo Street Runners • Gene Vincent

Barry James • Rickey Baron

Rob Storme and The Whispers

TOP 50 DISCS PLAYED AT THE GAUMONT AND MAJESTIC
— 1960-1965 —

Nutrocker	*B Bumble and the Stingers*
Baby Sitting Boogie	*Bobby Angelo*
Runaway	*Del Shannon*
I Remember You	*Frank Ifield*
Whole lot o' Shakin' Goin' on	*Jerry Lee Lewis*
Newcastle Twist (Who's Chicken)	*Lord Rockingham's XI*
Cotton Fields	*The Highwaymen*
Drumming up a Storm	*Sandy Nelson*
Walk on by (wait on the corner) or 'by the Town Hall'	*Leroy Van Dyke*
Picture of you	*Joe Brown*
Multiplication	*Bobby Darin*
Happy Birthday Sweet Sixteen	*Neil Sedaka*
Shout	*Lulu*
Half way to Paradise	*Billy Fury*
Take good care of my baby	*Bobby Vee*
Shakin' all over	*Johnny Kidd*
Apache	*The Shadows*
Peggy Sue	*Buddy Holly*
Sweets for my sweet	*The Searchers*
Glad all over	*The Dave Clarke Five*
Twist	*Chubby Checker*
Living Doll	*Cliff Richard*
Speedy Gonzales	*Pat Boone*
Breaking up is hard to do	*Neil Sedaka*
Blue Moon	*The Marcels*
Summer Holiday	*Cliff Richard*
5.4.3.2.1.	*Manfred Mann*
The House of the Rising Sun	*The Animals*
I Get Around	*The Beach Boys*
Sweet Little Sixteen	*Chuck Berry*
New Orleans	*Gary U.S. Bonds*
What'd I say	*Ray Charles*
Bits & Pieces	*The Dave Clarke Five*
C'mon Everybody	*Eddie Cochran*
The Wanderer	*Dion*
Shazam	*Duane Eddy*
Sherry	*The Four Seasons*
How do you do it	*Gerry and the Pacemakers*
Telstar	*The Tornados*
You really got me	*The Kinks*
Let's jump the broomstick	*Brenda Lee*
It's late	*Ricky Nelson*
Just one look	*The Hollies*
Dream Baby	*Roy Orbison*
Twenty four hours from Tulsa	*Gene Pitney*
Five foot two, eyes of blue	*Shane Fenton*
La Bamba	*Richie Valens*
Be-Bop-a-Lula	*Gene Vincent*
Rhythm of the falling rain	*Cascades*
The Locomotion	*Little Eva*

During these years the prolific hits of the following stars would be played at least two or three times a week: Elvis Presley, The Everly Brothers, Cliff Richard, Buddy Holly, Little Richard, The Beatles, and The Rolling Stones. These could always be included in any top fifty list.

116

EPILOGUE
The Local
Group Legend

As opposed to the single artist, a duo, trio, or four or more people made you a group. Most of our local groups were the usual four members consisting of drummer, bass guitarist, rhythm guitarist and lead guitarist. Of these, one would be the vocalist. In some cases a fifth member would be included specifically as the vocalist. His resposibility, apart from the obvious, was compering the act, introducing numbers and creating general conversation during the inevitable breaks between each number performed.

The many groups of the time copied the pop numbers and discs currently being played throughout the Rock 'n' Roll world. Some could perform the number with accuracy, others tried and failed. As one popular number faded, the next would be rehearsed and performed until that too outgrew its popularity. Others were kept in the repertoire as they would never die, notably: *Shakin' All Over, Whole lot o' Shakin' Goin' On, Johnny B Goode, Sweet Little Sixteen,* and for instrumental numbers, the indestructable *Apache.*

As capital was not forthcoming, most groups struggled along with very basic equipment. In some cases the group had just one amplifier whereas each individual guitarist should really have had his own. If no PA system was available the vocalist was in for a rough ride, trying to make himself heard over the guitars and general crowd reaction.

Guitars of the time were expensive and not readily available to the average working teenager, so it was inevitable that many group members created their own and although rough and ready most were ingeniously made with many attachments and could compare quite favourably with their expensive counterparts. The only drawback with the homemade guitars was that they occasionally gave off shocks, but no fatalities were ever recorded.

Dress was optional, but again, as the finance was not available groups were not able to dress as they would have wished. This was before the unkempt later Sixties. Most were well groomed young men wearing their best suit and tie. A standing joke at the time was to be on the same bill as the Cresters, especially at the Students' Club. The mediocre local group would perform first proudly dressed in their mix'n'match best suits together with their one amplifier and small hand mike, to be followed and completely outshone by the fabulous and very professional Cresters impeccably dressed, a clone of each other in their Group Suits, five or six Vox amplifiers, and the rest. It was then that we realised how mediocre the others really were. But it was all part of the game, and there was never any animosity, we were all good friends.

Transport was non-existant to most of the groups. Local buses conveyed members and equipment to the bookings. Engagements were contracted by the group members themselves, as only in a few cases did the local groups have a manager of sorts. Most information was passed on from group to group on where bookings were obtainable, what it was like and how much etc. This was the world of the local groups in the late Fifties and early Sixties . . .

Bradford Groups of the Early 1960s

In my introduction, and throughout the book, I have mentioned our very own local groups and celebrities. Some thanks should be extended to them for the pleasure they brought to our Rock 'n' Roll scene all those years ago. So, I have devoted the epilogue to them by showing original black and white photographs which capture the atmosphere of those days. Sadly, many others are not represented but, thanks to the few who have donated the pictures and their history, it will revive many memories for many middle-aged ex-fans.

To all of these a big Thankyou

Mick Sagar and The Cresters
The Dingos
The Del Rio Four
Lee Chevin and The Ravers
The Dave Lee Sound
The Tuxedos
Vince Wayne and The Falcons
Sansovinos
Dal Stevens and The Four Dukes
The Rhythm Rebels
Mel Clarke Four
Helen and The Tomboys
The Dakotas
Gary Lane and The Rockets
Geoff and The Prosecutors
Lorraine and The Bahtats
Robin Hood and His Merry Men
The Meteors
Rev Black and The Rocking Vickers
Joey White and The Blueknights
The Avengers
The Ravers
Clay Martin and The Trespassers
The Taledos
Mick Judge and The Jurymen
The Telecasters
The Delkados
Royalists
The Stormville Five
Dave Arran and The Crusaders
Brenda and The Dominators
Mick and The Tornadoes
Terry Sexton and The Shakes
The 789 Skiffle Group
Spike O'Brien and The Rattlers
Geoff and the Fairlanes
The Phantoms
Three Good Reasons
Branwell and The Brontebeats with Charolotte
The Tennasseans
The Four Musketeers

Carl Gresham

"Impressario"

Bradfordian Carl Gresham, like many of today's established impressarios, has a background steeped in show business. During the 1960s he appeared throughout Yorkshire fronting a pop group as a lead singer, and while he is the first to admit that his vocal qualities leave much to be desired, those appearances gave him the bug for the entertainment business. To earn extra cash he joined the list of many television companies' "extras", and found himself working in major television studios throughout the North, particularly with Granada who, through their constant rebooking of his services, eventually gave him the opportunity to meet up with many of the stars who today work through his promotional and management company. These include many famous personalities such as Morecambe and Wise, Pat Phoenix, Patrick Mower, Peter Wyngarde, Gordon Jackson, Frazer Hines, Dennis Waterman and international star Tony Curtis.

Many thanks were due to Carl for the numerous occasions he stepped in to look after the scene at the Majestic (see photo) whilst Dadio and myself were on holiday. Although we had different styles, Carl had his followers just as we had. Reliability and professionalism did not abound in those days, but Carl had both and still has to this day.

The late Pat Phoenix with Carl when he was acting as her agent. Pat had had an early affiliation with Bradford when working at the Bradford Playhouse.

Mike Sagar and the Cresters

MICHAEL SAGAR
HIS MASTER'S VOICE RECORDS

Probably Bradford's most well known top group of the Sixties. In October 1960 they recorded *Deep Feeling* at EMI Studios, London. On its release it was voted "a hit" on *Juke Box Jury* but failed to live up to its expectations. There were several theories why: bad management, failure of the record company to promote, even that they didn't produce sufficient copies of the record. Also, it was said the number wasn't popular with other groups who found it difficult to play, therefore no exposure!

Although still semi-professional in the early Sixties, they managed to perform at many engagements throughout the North — Kendel, Morecambe, Skegness, Bridlington. In the Summer of 1961 they played at the Old Queen's Theatre, Blackpool, being on the same bill as Emile Ford and John Leyton. Two girls joined the group at this time to augment the backing vocals, but left at

(1960-63) The Original Mike Sagar and The Cresters.
Colin Houghton, Drums; Malcolm Clark, Rhythm Guitar; Ian Bannister, Bass Guitar; Richard Harding, Lead Guitar.

the end of 1961 when the group turned professional and came under the agency of "Tommy Sanderson" who also managed the Barron Knights.

The Cresters were now playing venues nationwide, particularly in the London area, being based at a house in Kilburn.

Regrettably, Mike Sagar suffered from a throat problem which needed an operation, several months after which he needed to recover. In his absence the group continued as "The Cresters". During this time Richard Harding recorded two instrumentals for EMI *Temptation* and *Jezabel*. The record was released on the same day as the Everly Brothers' vocal version, result - no chance! Broadcasts followed with "NDO" Show from Manchester, two TV shows, *Talent Showcase* from London, and from Bristol (early 1963) the *Jimmy Young 6.25 Show* — incidentally, all live in those days. They also toured Stirling in Scotland where, at one particular venue, all the girls crowded around the stage when performing. This made the boys jealous so they threw coins at them causing the curtains to close.

Mike joined them again, but not for long. They had a disagreement and he stormed out of the digs in Kilburn, walked to Kilburn High Road, and thumbed a lift home to Yorkshire. He left the group from that time on. With low wages, incessant travelling, and the usual arguments, The Cresters of that time slowly parted.

The Local Boys
who nearly made it to the top

The late Colin Houghton, drummer, previously with many local groups was greatly respected by the pop world as a very talented performer. The late Malcolm Clark, rhythm guitarist, ex-Dingo (Roy Orbison vocals perfectly simulated). Mike Sagar, vocals, Bradford's male no 1 pop star of the time. Ian Bannister, bass guitarist, ex-Dingo. Lead guitar Richard Harding, regarded as one of the North's leading exponents of Rock 'n' Roll, admired by stars Carl Perkins and Chuck Berry. He did session work for other pop star performers. Time has not erased his reputation as one of the most skilled and original performers on the electric guitar.

For an insight into The Cresters of yesteryear, I am indebted to the late Colin Houghton who sadly passed away in 1989. Perhaps the above record will serve as a tribute to his enthusiasm of this era and memory of a fine fellow artiste.

The Dingos

After the Cresters, probably Bradford's best known Rock 'n' Roll group. From the early days of skiffle and into the Sixties this group brought to the area a very professional team and when they were joined by Garth B Cawood in the late Fifties, together with his managerial and entrep-

Dingo later addition: Dave Butterfield (1961), Bass Guitarist. Today Dave still takes his guitar around the world on business trips, taking part in sessions particularly in the States.

reneurial skills, the Dingos became a household name to the teenagers of Bradford. Names like Terry Moran, pianist (Ex Blue Jays) — later "Dadio" joining Dal as "Dal and Dadio". The late Malcolm Clark, rhythm guitarist, later became a member of the Cresters. Malcolm's rendering of Roy Orbison's *Crying* was magical: almost identical to the original. Sadly, Malcolm passed away still in his twenties, a sad loss to his many friends and admirers, leaving an underlying regret for what might have been. Ian Bannister, bass guitar, also, at a later stage, joined the Cresters. Kenny Fowler, lead guitar had a flair not unlike Carl Perkins. Drummer Irvin (Smudge) Smith, always cheerful and the envy of many other local drummers, rounded off what might have been a top recording group had not the inevitable split to other groups occurred.

The original Dingos, left to right: Terry (Dadio) Moran, Garth Cawood (note the maracas!), Malcolm Clark, Ian Bannister, Kenny Fowler, Irvin (Smudge) Smith.

Lee Chevin
and the Ravers

The first real break came after a chance in a million meeting with Russ Conway on the forecourt of a Bradford garage . The group stopped for petrol and saw Russ's Rolls-Royce convertible. Soon Russ had been told all about the group and a few weeks later Lee Chevin and the Ravers had passed an audition for George Martin (of Beatles fame) and in July 1963 made a record at the now famous Abbey Road Studios in London. The record was released in November 1963. The A-side was *Darling Jean* written by Bastow/Pannet coupled with *Memories of you* written by Chevin. The record was released on the Parlaphone EMI label. It was at this time the group had to change their name from "The Ravers" to "The Riders". The reason for the change was because of another recording group called "Paul Raven and the Ravers", who later became Gary Glitter and the Glitter Band. The recording engineer who worked on the disc was a guy called Norman Smith better known as "Hurricane Smith" who had one or two hits in the British charts. *Memories of you* was also recorded by the Applejacks who were Number One at the time with *Tell me when*. A song, *In love with an Angel* written by lead guitarist Rod Wright was put on disc by a singer called "Draffi" and released in Germany. The group was offered a five year contract by impressario Tito Burns who was the manager of Cliff Richard and The Shadows, Shirley Bassey and many many more stars, needless to say, the group signed.

From left to right: Dave Pannett, Brian Bastow, Rod Wright, Lee Chevin and Dave Archer.

Stars Lee Chevin and The Ravers appeared with

Lulu	Barron Knights
Manfred Mann	Vince Eager
Shane Fenton and The Fentones	Jess Conrad
Merseybeats	Mike Sarne *(Come outside)*
Applejacks	Mike Sagar and The Cresters
Pickwicks	Edna Savage

In 1968 the group were offered work in Germany but they had to have a girl singer as well as Lee Chevin. They auditioned one or two singers, but the girl who got the job was Pauline Matthews later to become Kiki Dee. The tour was called off before the start because Kiki was too young to go and had to pull out.

The Mel Clarke Four

I n April 1958 four young men entered a talent audition at Girlington Hall, Bradford, Guitarist/Singer Mel Hogan straight from grammar school; Bass Guitarist Steve (Red) Williams, a painter; Drummer Colin Houghton, with a transport company; and Peter Williams, rhythm guitar.

They were called at the time "The Unknown Four". After this audition Peter Williams dropped out and joined the Navy. He was replaced by a talented young pianist named Drew Charles. This turned out to be a step in the right direction. A pianist with a Rock 'n' Roll band in those days was indeed a rarity, as the usual line up was three guitars and drums, but what an asset Drew was! This quickly became apparent when he introduced his raw boogie blues influence to Mel's already Chuck Berry style guitar playing. This proved later to set the band aside as being different to the usual British sound emulated by most of the local groups.

After about six weeks of rehearsing together a letter arrived confirming that the band had passed the audition at Girlington and were to appear at St George's Hall, Bradford, a highly prestigious, if unpaid, venue where the top names in showbiz still perform.

Mel Clarke (16).
A pleasure to know and work with.

The much respected Drew Charles in the early 60s.
(30 years on and he's hardly changed!)

Telephone :
Shipley 52994 & 43508

THE "MEL CLARKE" FOUR
(Versatile Rhythm in Blues Combo)

The band performed three numbers, a guitar instrumental written for the occasion by Mel, called *Hauntin'*, a Chuck Berry number called *Johnny B Good* and a brilliant rendition by Drew of the Jerry Lee Lewis classic *Great Balls of Fire*. They came second and were no longer unknown. The name 'Unknown Four' was subsequently dropped. Mel Hogan became Mel Clarke and the Mel Clarke Four were born. The name of the show was *The Top Talent Show* and though the band never achieved the kind of fame available only to a few, they did become one of the handful of local bands to perform regularly at the Majestic Ballroom, The Gaumont, the Gaiety Ballroom, and the Students' Club.

The band played continuously from the late Fifties into the Sixties with almost the same line up, except for the drummers who were too numerous to recall, having lost the talented Colin Houghton in the early Sixties to the Tennesseans, later to became the Cresters who were turning professional and were making a record. The band did later cut three demo discs of their own at the Excel studios, two singles and an EP. The EP was taken by the local DJ Jimmy Saville (yes, now Sir James) to be plugged on his new radio venue, but was never taken up by the major record companies.

The Mel Clarke Four, along with other local bands such as The Cresters, The Dingos, The Mystics and many more, were also support bands for some of the top groups to come into the area, and travelled throughout Yorkshire and Lancashire appearing at such places as The Huddersfield Empire (Continental) for a full week's cabaret and at The Imperial Volume in Colne, a huge place and 'the' venue. All this despite the fact that the band had never had an agent and preferred to accept work as it came up. They sometimes worked five nights a week.

When the band finally broke up, Mel went to join the Dingos, Drew played with several different bands as he was in such demand he could pick and choose, Red gave up playing for a while, but all four of the original group are still playing. All are very privileged to have been part of a musical era that gave such enormous pleasure and warmth, not only to people listening but also to fellow artistes.

The Mel Clark Four: Mel, Drew, Colin, Red.

Helen
&
The Tomboys

O ne of the scarce female artistes of the time, seen here on stage with the Dingos at the Majestic, her stage name being "Dee Lawrence", later this was to change to her own name with her own group "Helen & The Tomboys". Again a sign of the times. Very popular and although some international status later, never quite made the top.

Helen McCaffrey

The
Avengers

The Avengers were formed in 1959, originally called the "Teenbeats" and played at the Majestic and Gaumont on regular occasions. They went professional in 1962 at Butlins Holiday Camp in Bognor Regis but disbanded shortly afterwards.

From left to right: Ernest Foster, Jimmy Boocock, Johnnie Casson (Drummer) and Geoff Barnes.

Johnnie Casson went on to join The Cresters in 1963. Again here was a superb drummer who could have filled any slot with any top star group of the time. He is still in demand today and is a national television/cabaret star.

Clay Martin and The Trespassers

Paul Hornby and Allan Davies were the originators of Clay Martin and the Trespassers. Having both attended the same school, Carlton Grammar, and also living opposite each other, at the age of 14 they formed a Skiffle group, consisting of a tea-chest bass and acoustic guitar. Playing at local church halls and youth clubs, they were next joined by Steve Clayton on drums. Barry Clay and Kevin, soon also became members of this up and coming group. The Trespassers became quite popular in the next few months, playing at pubs, working men's clubs and local dance halls such as The Majestic, The Gaumont and The Queens at Idle.

Following the usual arguments that took place within most groups at that time, Barry Clay left to be replaced by Rita, a female singer somewhat older than other members of the group. So the group changed their name to The Great Pacifics with Rita. Although the group was very popular, things were never quite the same and the group went their separate ways in August 1963.

From left to right: Paul Hornby, lead guitar, vocals; Steve Clayton, drums; Barry Clay, lead vocals; Kevin, rhythm guitar, vocals; Allan Davies, bass guitar, vocals.

The
Royalists

The Royalists began as a resident group playing at the Victoria Hotel, Park Lane, Bradford in 1963. One of the originators of this group was Allan Davies, formally of Clay Martin and The Trespassers. The Royalists soon became popular as a backing group for various local singers. One of these was Malcolm Murray. Murray joined the band on a permanent basis, quickly followed by the new drummer Vic Storey. They worked for TV enterprises for about three months before going to Butlins at Minehead in Somerset for a Summer Season in 1964. Later in September of that year they went to London to record for Johnny Silver who worked for Thames Television, but due to family problems they returned home in November and began playing the Club and Cabaret scene until the following April, 1965 when again they were contracted to Butlins Holiday Camp, this time in Filey. After the Summer Season, they were fixed up with a tour of Germany but unfortunately this fell through and the band returned to the local scene. Gradually in the following months the group members dispersed and the group sadly split up.

The Royalists (Butlins, Filey, 1965)
Left to right: Malcolm (Mac) Murray, lead vocals; Vic Storey, drums; Allan Davies, bass guitar, vocals; Roy Bould, piano and vocals. Note the Selma pianatron keyboard (early days).

The Crusaders

One of Bradford's more successful groups during 1960-63. After the finish of Dal Stevens & The Four Dukes, Keith (Drums) and Dennis (Vocal) went on to join up with Clifford Dutton (Rhythm Guitar), Henry Rhodes (Lead Guitar) and Norman Sutcliffe (Bass Guitar) to form the Crusaders, who later had a successful couple of years on the local scene, at one stage having Pauline Matthews (Kiki Dee) in the line up. Dennis eventually left, to be replaced by Dave Arran (Vocal) from the Dakotas, and the group continued until it was decided to try a spot of work in Germany. Keith left the group prior to departure for Germany in 1963, and teamed up again with Dennis (Bass Guitar/Vocal) and recruited Dave Biven (Rhythm Guitar/Vocal) and Paul Flintoft (Lead Guitar/Vocal) to form the Four Musketeers, who worked on the club circuit until mid 1965, when the group dis-banded.

Left to Right: Keith Artist, drums; Dennis 'Duane' Oliver, vocal; Henry Rhodes. lead Guitar; Cliff Dutton, rhythm guitar; Norman Sutcliffe, bass guitar.

Mick
and the
Tornadoes

Extremely popular during Bradford's Rock 'n' Roll era. Mick Kershaw and the Tornadoes performed at almost every venue during these years. Versatility and outright professionalism ensured this group was consistently popular; especially from the female fans point of view where Mick Kershaw's good looks could compete with any of the famous 'Budding Bobbies' and 'Rocking Rickies' of the time.

The group was occasionally mistaken for The Tornados of Telstar fame, the letter E being the only difference in the name. With polish and perfection augmented by their brilliant lead guitarist Ian (Chunky) Normington, this group survived many of its contempories until the mid-1960s.

Mick and the Tornadoes 1960-1965.
Left to right: Dave Murgatroyd, Dave Gallagher, Mick Kershaw, Mick Stevenson, Ian (Chunky) Normington.

Terry Sexton
and
The Shakes

Terry had a self supporting group, having his own van. They were one of the few groups who had a female vocalist, Diana Stevens. Diana sang for the group in the beginning for free, as no-one thought that she was good enough to be paid. Glamour, however, helped their image, and after twelve months, she was put on the payroll. The group did pass auditions for Butlins and Continental Tours, but they could not persuade one or another of their band members to go. (A usual occurance of the time).

Around 1965 the band broke up. Diana auditioned for a Mecca band at York, and soon after joined The Ivor Kenny Band, who were the Mecca band of the year for a few years running. So much for the groups judgement of a few years earlier! Terry Sexton and the Shakes were, however, remembered as being one of the more professional groups of that era.

Terry Sexton and The Shakes.
Rear: Raymond Smith, Brian Fillingham, Dave Wiggins, Mick Stephenson.
Centre: Terry Sexton and Diana Stevens.

The 789
Skiffle Group

In their early days as a local Bradford group they practised in a front living room. This was the usual pattern for most group members. The next step was to graduate to Rock 'n' Roll, hoping for fame and fortune!

The 789 Skiffle Group (1958).
Left to right: Brian Leek, rhythm guitar and vocals; Keith Artist, washboard; Brian Foster, tea chest bass; Tony Gribbin, lead guitar.

"Spike" O'Brien
Piano and Keyboard Genius

After experience with the Rhythm Rebels, Spike became a member of the Dingos (one of the originals). He formed his own group in 1963 called The Rattlers completing three successful seasons in Douglas, Isle of Man (first British band in the island). Later he joined Don Partridge (the one man band) in his backing group The Wild Fowl. In 1973 Spike recorded *Poor Little Fred* (skit on *Big Bad John*) which had moderate success. In the 1990s Spike is still touring Bradford circuits with local groups and is as popular now as he was in the 60s when his name and talent were the subject of much envy and discussion among the other groups.

Garth Cawood

Disc Jockey ... Artiste ...
Compere ... Entrepreneur ...

I t could be said that Garth was probably one of the earliest ballroom DJs in the UK. He began at the Tudor Ballroom, Dudley Hill in the mid 1950s, where he used an old type (modern then) radiogramme, which held eight discs (78s). During the thirty second automatic change, Garth would give some type of introduction. Primitive, but it worked, therefore becoming the forerunner of the modern disco DJ.

In the late 1950s he joined the Dingos, who were established as a local skiffle group. Garth had seen them on stage at the old Roxy Cinema and while they were quite talented, their organisation and professionalism was not so hot. For example, at the end of each number played, there was no thank you or introduction into the next number. Garth's arrival turned the Dingos Skiffle group into probably one of the most professional and entertaining groups

THE POP IDOL
(Note the maracas)

in the area. Garth's other contribution was to front the group as compere together with an occasional vocal. Like myself, Garth could not play an instrument, consequently our memories of him on stage evoke the image of an impeccably dressed young man, white gloves to boot, accompanying the group shaking the maracas or tambourine.

After a few years the group folded and its members went their different ways, some to join other groups and others to semi-retirement. Garth with his usual

THE SHOWMAN

flair as the showman took over the Top Twenty at Idle and staged shows starring many of the pop stars who had previously appeared at the Majestic and Gaumont.

Into the 1960s he was soon compering package shows throughout the UK, being on first name terms with the Beatles and the Stones. After spending five years in St Tropez organising and entertaining the wealthy, he returned to Bradford where he again became a variety agent, as well as still compering shows and having his own DJ spot on Pennine Radio.

Today Garth is acknowledged throughout showbusiness circles as a leading variety agent and entrepreneur. Some things change, but Garth Cawood is still the enthusiastic and professional showman I knew in Bradford's Rock 'n' Roll era of the Fifties and Sixties.

The Del Rio Four

Anotable group of the Fifties and Sixties was The Del Rio Four, who, like their compatriots, made the rounds of dance halls and clubs and the odd season at Butlins. Within a few years the majority of the group were to leave and join other prominent local groups, but the mainstay of this group was the vocalist, Ray Kennan, whose career demands to be recorded. Ray's on-stage exhibitions pervaded nearly every aspect of his life. In a recent lucid moment he revealed that in his capacity as group newsmaker, many of his outrageous tales were greatly exaggerated for publicity's sake, others pure fabrication; e.g. setting fire to the piano during one performance. But the claim regarding driving a van through double locked doors into a club, being the only way of entry, was quite true. Though his antics necessitated extreme sanctions from whichever group he was with at the time, his assets were considered far greater than any liabilities, a judgement born out later by performances with many international artistes.

Ray, a Bingley lad, (almost a day trip away from Bradford in those days), joined the Belvardos as vocalist in 1959, followed by a brief spell with the Deepbeats. In 1960 he joined The Del Rio Four as vocalist/compere, with whom he played a season at Butlins. On leaving this group an assortment of changes took place: The Ray Kennan Combo, The Taledos, The Quiet Three, and then a ten piece rock 'n' roll group called The Governors. This was supplemented by his job as a

The Del Rio Four.
Left to right: Martin Kershaw, Kenny Gough, Ray Kennan and Malcolm Ives.

petrol pump attendant and local joinery work. Back as a single vocalist compere, he toured with Lulu, the Rolling Stones, Manfred Mann and Screaming Lord Sutch. Shows followed at the then famous Eden Saloon in Berlin with Sammy Davies Jnr., Jerry Lee Lewis and Johnny Cash. *Its Not Unusual* to know that in the early Sixties, Tom Jones, an unknown quantity then, spent some time working with Ray. It's hard to imagine the scene now; Ray Kennan and Tom Jones in the 'phone box (still there) at Ferncliffe Road in Bingley chasing bookings! Ray used that 'phone box as his office. He went on to compere shows, one of his last being a major triumph, when he took Blackpool by storm. As second billing to P.J. Proby the inevitable happened, Proby failed to turn up to perform at the North Pier and Ray was asked to take over. His stage presence, experience, and easy singing style more than compensated the disappointed Proby fans. With the world seemingly now his oyster, with his usual unpredictability, he cooly packed his tent and stole away. He had had enough.

The Phantoms

The Phantoms were formed in 1962 by four typical teenagers of the time. In a short period they developed into one of the top groups in Yorkshire, taking second place in the *Melody Maker* poll of Yorkshire groups. At the same time they won the prestigious Northern Song Contest at St. George's Hall. Their gimmick at this time was to have their hair bleached (something almost unheard of in those days). A change came about with Colin Whitley taking the place of Roy Waterworth (Bass). At the same time they changed from 'the Phantoms' to the very local sounding name of 'Branwell and the Brontebeats with Charlotte'. Charlotte was local girl Ann McCormack, and they all wore traditional clothing of the Bronte period. After 12 months of touring in a converted forty-two seater coach, the group folded. Peter Clegg, Ann McCormack, Danic (Danny) Radivoj then formed 'The Three Good Reasons' who soon gained a recording contract with Phillips on the Murcury label. Their first single *Build Your Love* unfortunately was not a hit, but some success followed with a number one hit in Holland with a track from the beatles album *Nowhere Man!* After their third single release *Moment of Truth* written by Marty Wilde, The Three Good Reasons parted, leaving their mark locally, and in Holland.

The Three Good Reasons
Left to right: Danic (Danny) Radivoj, Ann McCormack, Peter Clegg.
A number one hit in Holland.

The Phantoms
Left to right: Brindley Jardine, drums; Chris Gibson, lead guitar; Peter Clegg, rhythm guitar; Roy Waterworth, bass guitar.

Index

Index

Index

All Our Yesterdays 1988

Left to right: Dennis (Duane) Oliver, Keith Artist, Mel Clarke, Dal Stevens, Drew Charles.